ENGLAND & AMERICA

LECTURES DELIVERED ON THE
SIR GEORGE WATSON FOUNDATION
FOR AMERICAN HISTORY, LITERATURE,
AND INSTITUTIONS

1921 VISCOUNT BRYCE
1922 ARTHUR TWINING HADLEY
1923 NICHOLAS MURRAY BUTLER
1924 ALBERT FREDERICK POLLARD
1925 SIR ROBERT FALCONER
1926 ROBERT McELROY
1927 CLAUDE H. VAN TYNE

ENGLAND & AMERICA

Rivals in the American Revolution

by

CLAUDE H. VAN TYNE

Head of Department of History
University of Michigan

CAMBRIDGE
AT THE UNIVERSITY PRESS
1927

CAMBRIDGE
UNIVERSITY PRESS

University Printing House, Cambridge CB2 8BS, United Kingdom

Published in the United States of America by Cambridge University Press, New York

Cambridge University Press is part of the University of Cambridge.

It furthers the University's mission by disseminating knowledge in the pursuit of education, learning and research at the highest international levels of excellence.

www.cambridge.org
Information on this title: www.cambridge.org/9781107645295

© Cambridge University Press 1927

First published 1927
First paperback edition 2014

A catalogue record for this publication is available from the British Library

ISBN 978-1-107-64529-5 Paperback

PREFACE

Sir George Watson, the founder of the chair which makes possible these lectures on American History and Institutions, was doubtless well aware of the prevailing English indifference, even aversion, to study of the life and past experiences of the great republic of the New World. Perhaps he did not fully appreciate the difficulty of making the British public drink at the Pierian spring. Whatever his vision or amiable delusion, he did a noble thing in a generous way, and hoped, as do all idealists, for a great attainment. At the present day, however, a vastly greater number of Americans are listening with interest to what English lecturers are saying about British history and imperial problems than there are Englishmen who care to try to understand the historical past and national problems of America. There must be a greater parity in the efforts to comprehend each other, if the two great English-speaking peoples are ever to reach that mutual understanding in which all men of vision see the best hope of world peace and democratic progress.

If the British public listens only to a senatorial voice from Idaho, or an even more strident one from Missouri, it may well conclude that America has profited little from the efforts of English scholars and publicists to explain their Empire, but any of those visitors to the American academic centres can assure their countrymen of the great predominance there of sympathetic and understanding persons. It is chiefly among the ignorant masses, or certain unforgiving racial groups, that one finds the two maddening convictions—one, that the British Empire never ceases its efforts to regain its lost American provinces, and the second, that settled delusion that Americans dwell on a sanctified isle in the midst of a wild and godless sea. Yet there is one other source of the latter idea. People in England should remember that, except for a comparatively few intellectuals and observing travellers, the United States is still a land under the influence of the westward movement. One hundred and fifty years ago, three million people faced millions of square miles of unexploited lands, forests, mining regions, stretching away from the Atlantic to the Pacific. Their faces turned from Europe to this absorbing task. Picture them, generation after generation, moving up the valleys, over the mountains, beyond the Mississippi, through the Rockies. About them were the crashing forests, the wide prairies, the hidden treasures of the mountains. They forgot Europe, they saw only the task before them. Hardly a generation ago was that work near enough completion for them to take breath. Not yet have they time to think of the old world—behind them. Their politicians, if not as ignorant as they, at least use the easiest arguments with them. It is easier to talk of local, home problems, and they urge men to forget "abroad." We know that in the Middle Ages men imagined the Atlantic as a Sea of Darkness. If one ventured far out on that sea, one would encounter sea-monsters, writhing serpents, wicked dragons, that destroyed men. We are not wholly rid of that idea to-day. It is still easy for American politicians to picture the Atlantic as a Sea of Darkness, to make men imagine that if they cross it they will find over there European statesmen, terrible monsters, intriguing wicked fellows waiting to devour our innocent diplomats and statesmen who venture there. Did not one of these monsters recently go so far as to invite a senator to visit him? This vague fear of Europe helps to explain our aloofness, American complacency. Give us time and this will pass away. Exchanges of ideas, education of both nations as to the institutions of both, and tolerance for what we do not understand, will, I am sure, cement that friendship, which it was the purpose of the founder of this chair to further.

The lectures presented in this volume are based upon some twenty-five years of study and investigation in the field of the American Revolution. The opinions are my own, but are often based upon the conclusions drawn by the writers of famous monographs, the results of years of investigation by distinguished scholars. No one can write now upon the subject of the merchants' interests and the economic causes of the American Revolution without recourse to the work of A. M. Schlesinger, C. M. Andrews, and George Louis Beer. One cannot treat properly the political and constitutional aspects until one reads Carl Becker, Andrew C. McLaughlin, J. F. Jameson and C. W. Alvord. On the whole subject of the Revolution and its background, one must not neglect Osgood and Channing. There are many minor obligations of this nature which the limitations of space and the absence of footnotes forbid me to mention.

I cannot express my gratitude to each university head and to every particular officer or professor in the several universities, who made my stay there one of the greatest social pleasures that I have ever enjoyed, nor can I in this stage of America's intellectual and social development go quite so far in the warmth of my admiration as did Benjamin Franklin before his heart was seared by Wedderburn's insolence. "Of all enviable things," he wrote, "I envy England most its people. Why should that petty island which...is but like a stepping-stone in a brook, scarce enough of it above water to keep one's shoes dry...enjoy in almost every neighbourhood more sensible, virtuous and elegant minds than we can collect in ranging a hundred leagues of our vast forests." America, too, in our age has its many "sensible virtuous, and elegant minds" of whose existence I found many of my delightful hosts fully aware. One who is wholly American at heart, and who wishes to be nought else, can only say that there is a charm and elegance and finish about English society which gives to England one of its most enviable distinctions.

C. H. VAN TYNE

August 4, 1927

CONTENTS

xi

Lecture I

THE STRUGGLE FOR THE TRUTH ABOUT THE AMERICAN REVOLUTION

Last year was the sesquicentennial of the Declaration of Independence. So important was it regarded that we Americans, as a nation, stopped, even in the midst of the flood of gold that poured over us, and showed considerable sentiment about that historical event. There were celebrations, fairs, new books on the Revolution, new orations, and even new poets burst into song. June 7th of this notable year marked the 150th anniversary of the time when Richard Henry Lee rose in the Continental Congress and moved that "these united colonies are, and of a right ought to be free and independent states." War had already begun, and it grew in bitterness, as the months and years wore on, until the treaty of peace of 1783 accomplished the end at which Congress aimed. From that time to this, historians have sought to learn what really happened.

There were, of course, conflicting English and American interpretations of the events, different appraisements of credit and blame. Strangely enough the historians of the opposing nations have had little trouble in coming to approximate agreements, and they can to-day discuss all the vital questions in a most harmonious spirit. The great conflict has been between popular tradition and the results of scholarly research. As in the warfare between religion and science the mass mind showed amazing powers of resistance to the charms of pure reason. Anatole France was very nearly right when he said that "if you present history in an unexpected aspect you surprise the reader, but he does not like to be surprised. If you try to instruct him, you only humiliate and anger him.... As a result an original historical view is an universal object of suspicion and disgust."

Yet not alone against this human trait have scholars fought, almost in vain, but against a much more sinister force, the interest of certain racial groups in keeping alive the old, unreasoning hate of England. Supporting these groups are all born fundamentalists who hold that a foundation stone of American patriotism, as firm as Plymouth Rock, is that we must not let die the old tradition about barbarous British "redcoats," a tyrannical King George, and a wicked Lord North. They cry out against reshaping the history of the Revolution "sacredly enshrined in the hearts of a free people

for a century and a half." They warn Americans
that this is being done "to serve international
interests, under whose hypnotism of propaganda
American public opinion has been goosestepping
for some years in the direction of a return to
British subjection." In the long struggle for the
truth about the American Revolution, progress
has been steadily resisted inch by inch by these
sturdy patriots. No appeal to reason or historical
sources seems to reach them. They appear to think
that the only way to get historical truth is to listen
to the war cries which sounded in the ears of the
fathers. Robert Ingersoll used to say that in every
mind was the little flame of reason, and before
each new thought, unfamiliar to his hearers, he
used to make the appeal: "Let the little flame
burn." In appealing to fundamentalists we can
have little hope that they will give the flame a
chance.

For nearly one hundred years after the awakening of the "spirit of '76" the story of the Revolution was told much as the contemporaries had told
it, bitterly, with no effort to be impartial or judicial,
and no emphasis upon the fundamentals. Men
like Bancroft conducted amazing researches in the
archives, but rose out of heaps of musty records
only to write again of the cunning, malevolent

King George and his wicked minister, Lord North, enemies of the human race, oppressors of America. In Bancroft's pages the worthy loyalists, Bernard and Hutchinson, "intrigue" and "work in the dark." Over against these villains of the play he set the intrepid patriot, the high-minded and simple-hearted Samuel Adams, and the god-like Patrick Henry, "forest-born Demosthenes." In Bancroft's view the Americans of 1776 were all "chosen to keep guard over the liberties of mankind." "While the earth was wrapped in gloom, they welcomed the daybreak of popular freedom and looked undazzled into the beams of the morning." He seemed to have forgotten Cromwell, Pym and Hampden, the luminous pages of Locke or Milton, or the prophets of all eighteenth-century revolution, Montesquieu, Rousseau. He forgot that English history is the most complete record of "freedom slowly broadening from precedent to precedent" in the annals of human evolution.

But even Bancroft was a mild Jingo. Ninety-three years after the Battle of Lexington, Hudson could solemnly write in his *History of Lexington*,

The towering obelisk on Bunker Hill which looks down in an awful frown upon British vandalism and in pious veneration upon American valor, the

4

modest shaft at West Cambridge which bespeaks alike the barbarity of the retreating foe and the heroic gathering of the friends of freedom, ready to do and suffer in her cause; the humble monument at Lexington proclaiming the undaunted firmness of the minute men and the cowardly spirit of the invaders of their rights.

There you have side by side British vandalism, barbarity and cowardice, and American valour, heroism, and undaunted firmness. On such historical pabulum were our fathers fed and even some of us in our youth.

After the great centennial celebration in 1876 there was a renewal of interest in American history. The *Magazine of American History* was founded. Historical societies sprang into being, some of them *not* for the purpose of concealing historical information. Sons and daughters of the Revolution created societies with membership so numerous as to reflect great credit on the ingenuity of genealogists who for a consideration would trace one's ancestral line unerringly back to some revolutionary soldier or other. In many cases an amazing horticultural skill was shown in making two ancestors grow where only one grew before. Another popular kind of increased interest was that shown in colonial furniture—a desire to acquire it, antedating that great access of acquisitiveness induced by the activities of the Sage of Dearborn. Finally, for the first time professors of American history began to appear in American schools and colleges, and here and there a scholar, an investigator.

It was these trained investigators who began to get at the truth as to the Revolution. With no aim but to understand, with no desire but to know the truth they worked for forty years—as long as the Chosen People searched for the Promised Land—rewriting the story of the founding of the American Republic. New records, new points of view, new principles of research made new generations of investigators see the Revolution in a new way. Many only tuned the instruments of the historical muse, that others might play that had better hands. They made keys to the archives, uncovered unknown records, collected great stores of revolutionary pamphlets and newspapers. They published reliable editions of the letters and the works of the Fathers. Washington was rescued from the pious efforts of Sparks to edit away his grammatical slips and his honest explosions of anger and disgust with "the summer soldier and the sunshine patriot." Famous monographs were written on the British commercial policy as an economic cause of revolution, on the Mississippi valley and its relation to the causes of the War of Independence, on the colonial merchants and their part in severing the empire, on the great differences in political theory which caused the colonials and the rulers of Great Britain to think different political thoughts to a point where they doubted each other's sincerity. The committee system, local and provincial, was studied, and its great influence shown in organizing the revolutionary forces, and guiding them to ultimate success. The Loyalists came into their own, the naturalness of their attitude, the nobility of their characters in many cases, the sincerity and justness of their contentions. In a word, histories of the Revolution ceased to be mere eulogy of heroes, a story of "disastrous chances," "moving incidents by flood and field," or mere catalogues of the forgotten, and became studies of the origin and growth of American institutions, honest efforts to learn the truth of a great epoch in the world's history. Historical facts and personages were put under a microscope rather than on a pedestal.

Consequent upon all this activity in research, professors of history in the great universities and colleges began to dare to give less attention to the

military, personal, and political sides of the
Revolution, and to talk of the mutating systems
of land-holding, shifting paths of commerce, the
new arteries through which American thought
and feeling flowed, and the modified relations of
social classes to each other. They talked to their
students of the march of social, economic and
political principles instead of the march of armed
men. It was not considered extra hazardous to
distinguish between the noble heroes like Washington who, with his devoted followers, actually
did endure all that cold, ache, penury, misrepre-
sentation could heap on life, and the less heroic
American masses, the greater number of whom
were reluctant to fight, wanting in decision, un-
willing to sacrifice for the great cause. College
students with three hours' credit dangling before
their eyes have been known to manifest no
riotous spirit even when told that in a country
containing something like 700,000 men of fighting
age, there was never, even on paper, over one-
eighth that number in state militia and Continental
army together, and that Washington was never
able to gather for any one battle over 20,000 men.
As a result of such indifference, and the conduct
of his subordinates, even Washington could be
reduced to such despair as to write,

Such a dearth of public spirit, and want of virtue, such stock-jobbing and fertility in all the low arts to obtain advantages of one kind or another.... I never saw before and I pray God I may never be witness to again.... Such dirty, mercenary spirit pervades the whole that I would not be at all surprised at any disaster that may happen.

And Ebenezer Huntington, fighting "the Lord's battles," as he firmly believed, wrote that he had lain in filthy rags for forty hours on the rain-soaked ground, while his countrymen, safe at home, held their purse strings as though they would "damn the world" rather than part with a dollar to save the country. As we read the records we come to realize that noble as was the example of patriotic sacrifice in that dreary, frozen, starving camp at Valley Forge, those ills were suffered because the farmers of the neighbourhood preferred British gold to paper "not worth a Continental," and the American people at home did not support the war nor the heroic army with the devotion shown north and south in 1861, and even more ardently by the whole country in 1918. Indeed, we fully agree with the opinion that, considering the nation in the mass, and not particular revolutionary heroes, the patriotism of 1861 was more diffused and ardent than that of 1776, and only nine years

9

ago we all saw a patriotism more general, more pure and more informed than that of either 1776 or 1861. Views like Washington's and Huntington's are distressing things to learn from unimpeachable sources; but historians are not cultivating the flowers of rhetoric; they are digging for the gold of truth.

Nor were these truths the most startling things which research made it compulsory to say. Professors, protected by their armoured tanks of academic freedom of speech, began to tell classes and even to write into textbooks, that George III was not a tyrant and his ministers not monsters, but rather mere victims of the economic theories of their age, and of the dominating convictions as to the duties of rulers toward subjects. Professors, who valued truth more than popularity, even declared that the Revolution was the finest fruit of the Englishman's long struggle for political liberty, that it was the glory of England that she had colonists who so mastered her own principles that they would rise to open rebellion if their ideas of liberty were profanely touched. They even asserted, that the freest of colonists were the first to rebel, that only English colonists in that age had such a conception of freedom as to snuff the taint of tyranny and to resort to revolution under no greater provocation than that which England had given them. Finally, in a fine frenzy, growing quite reckless of what Solons, dependent upon certain racial constituencies, might protest in the halls of Congress, scholars proclaimed that much of the traditional ill-feeling against Great Britain was groundless, that history revealed not barbarous cruelty and tyrannous oppression, but divergent influences that shaped the ends to which each country, England and America, was moving, that each had its auspicious destiny, each its noble past. Americans, starting with an English-born political philosophy, developed, in a new environment, new ways of attaining the freedom at which that philosophy aimed. Historical chance and varied environment created different methods of attaining and enjoying political liberty which proved fatal to political union and resulted in alienation and war. The British Empire, doomed to be broken asunder, was brought to that disaster by the insistent demand of Englishmen in America for the full enjoyment there of those liberties which England had fostered beyond any other country in the world. Principles for which English heroes had given their lives, Otis, Adams, Washington and Jefferson carried onward to a new goal, a new attainment in political liberty. It was best, doubtless, for the highest good of free institutions in the world that each idea should freely work out its logical destiny. Each system has its merits, each its disadvantages, but liberty has made advances under both.

Still another subject which for over one hundred years received no fair consideration was that of the loyalists, whom even the judicious Washington had called "those abominable pests of society." A calm study of the facts revealed that in New England, when war broke, a half at least of the wealthy, educated, and respected classes belonged to that party. Most of the great property owners of New York embraced it. Quakers and the great majority of Episcopalians, except in the south, did likewise. The richest farmers tended to take the royalist side. The most prosperous lawyers and physicians chose to support the king. In a word the culture, the dignity, the official rank, the inheritors of wealth tended to uphold the old order. Besides the fact observed in all ages that the prosperous tend to desire to preserve that *régime* which brought them prosperity, it must be remembered that they and the privileged classes were the very people to whom the dream of empire would most appeal. They conjured up a vision of an English-speaking people dominating the sea, the vast resources of India, the sea-board and the fertile interior valleys of America. Imagination pictured for them a world empire, rivalled by none, paramount over all, mingling everything that was best of west and east, a noble dominion, bringing peace, freedom and industrial growth over all the globe. It was this gorgeous prospect which they refused to abandon for an iridescent dream of independence and perhaps wild disorder.

While the Virginia aristocracy, dwelling apart on secluded estates far from the conservative influence of royal officers, and fired with a desire for local independence, were found on the Whig side, yet that was not true of the majority of the aristocracy in New England and the Middle States. The Revolution was on the whole the work of the lower and middle classes. Also youth espoused rebellion, age tended to cling to the old, or at least go slowly. A statistical study of the leaders, military and political, of the movement, reveals that fifty per cent., even of this upper crust, came of the middle and lower classes. Exceptions, like Washington and Hancock, there were, of course, but in general the strength of the revolutionary party lay in the plain people. Loyalists were ever railing against "the noisy, blustering and bellowing patriots," whom they called "the refuse and dregs of mankind." They sneered at the growing tendency to give the vote "to every biped of the forest," and resented the "Lycurguses, and Solons, in every coffee house, tavern and gin shop" in the land. The Whigs in their turn denounced the Loyalists as the rich, the titled, the haughty betrayers of the cause of America, and called attention to the fact that in the humbler ranks of the party were a remarkable number of chaise-makers, portrait painters, jewellers, goldsmiths and lapidaries, whose best trade came from aristocrats, the rich officials, wealthy merchants. Thus mutual recriminations furnished the best of unconscious evidence of the general truth of the character of the two parties. Certain we are that the states at the close of the war came to be ruled by lower classes than those which held the reins before the war.

In addition to entertaining these new views of the main features of the Revolution, teachers of history gleaned from the works of the critical scholars some corrected versions of minor events and episodes of the Revolution. One could apply the common rules of fair discussion even to the "redcoats," and tell, with apologies, that even they did courageous and generous things in the war. Describing the battle of Bunker Hill it might be cautiously suggested that "British pluck at last prevailed," rather than that "the cowardly British came up the hill the third time." Impartial study made it clear that British prisoners-of-war in American hands fared quite as badly as American prisoners in British prison hulks. It could be hinted that Ethan Allen, at Ticonderoga, instead of demanding a surrender in the name of the great Jehovah and the Continental Congress—from neither of which he had a commission—more likely said, "Come out of that, you d—d old rat!" Critical study even made one doubt the beautiful legends clinging about the Liberty Bell. Forty years ago, indeed, all professional historians knew that the Declaration of Independence was not signed on the fourth day of July. And all these results of the search after truth, were told, up to ten years ago, freely and fearlessly by all sincere students and teachers of history. Like the sons and daughters of Abyssinia, they wandered in the gardens of fragrance and slept on the fortresses of security. Up to the time of our entrance into the Great War there was a general feeling among scholars that the cause of truth had won some great victories. The only disquieting factor in the situation was the amazing resistance revealed by the popular mind to the inoculation of new ideas, resistance to the efforts of scholars to substitute truth for tradition. During forty years for example the truth about the time of signing the Declaration of Independence has been taught in every university and first class college in America, but were you to go out on the avenue to-day and ask the first hundred persons you meet, ninety-nine would tell you that it was signed, of course, on the fourth day of July. We learn from the poet that

Error wounded writhes with pain, and dies among her worshippers,

but the cynic comments, "She takes her time about it." On the William L. Clements Library at Ann Arbor there is an inscription which reads, "Tradition fades, but the written record remains ever fresh." Quite the reverse is true, for all my experience convinces me that tradition is about the most ineradicable thing in the human mind.

In the particular case of the Declaration signing, it makes little difference, except for the sake of accuracy, whether one has the true or traditional conception, but upon many other historical questions the acceptance of tradition rather than the truth will determine that a person will be a bigot rather than a tolerant, liberal citizen of the world.

Nevertheless, this curious trait of the human mind was only a shadow on the bright outlook for replacing error and prejudice with historical truth, but as the Great War neared its end, and with ever increasing volume thereafter, heavy clouds darkened the whole landscape in the province of history. The storm of propaganda swept over us, cowing the weak, amazing even the strong. Sinister demagogues, wild-eyed zealots, busybodies and nobodies, representing racial constituencies, patriotic societies, and labour organizations clamoured for history written and taught for their ends only. The daughters of the Dove of Peace and the sons of the Olive Branch pussy-footed up and down the land demanding that wars should not be mentioned in our histories, while the lords of the Dreadnought, and the children of the Fiery Dragon insisted upon more space for the ordeal by battle. Historians suddenly learned to their dismay that great and powerful societies, some arrogating to themselves great social prestige, cared nothing for the fine gold of historical truth, but preferred the dross of propaganda. Scholars were startled by cut-throat bandits in the path of research who demanded "Hands up! pass over the jewels of truth so recently discovered." Out in the Golden West where all loyal citizens admit that the mountains meet the sea, the library committee of San José banished from the city library a book on the American Revolution which a whole generation had read and studied with peaceful minds until grim-visaged war sharpened their scent for treason literature. Then Congressmen, with a singular perception of the value of limelight, attacked other books which had lain undisturbed on dusty shelves for twenty years. They filled pages of the Congressional Record with stirring rhetoric about "hands palsied by apologies, fettered by fees," which had "desecrated the tombs of American history." The historian was accused, like Socrates, of making new gods and denying the existence of old ones. Professors, wondering what they would do when the rent came 'round, found themselves credited with hoards of British gold covertly acquired. They had in fact about as much success in getting British gold as did Julius Caesar 1900 years before. Those who have read Cicero know the degree of his success.

In the main, these modern heresy hunters were too profoundly ignorant to know the books of the *great* heretics, the writers of famous monographs, of critical histories, who had been the real revisers of traditional opinions. Their shallow

pates were equal only to the examination of textbooks or rather to seizing upon isolated sentences
in them which shocked their historical funda-
mentalism. These texts, lagging a generation
behind the works of the real investigators, were
merely more judicious, more subdued in tone, less
free with praise and blame, because they embodied
the results of two generations of a search for truth.
For the first time the textbooks were being written
by scholars and specialists, not by journalists, needy
preachers, and professors of rhetoric, who read the
ancient tales and re-wrote them without reflection.

The first great attack upon the new and better
textbooks began, soon after the war, in the organs
of a great newspaper king, who for weeks devoted pages to reckless denunciation of all the
better school histories. Then this prince of the
muck-rakers wrote a letter to the mayor of New
York, asking for an investigation of the school
texts used there, and that learned and discrimin-
ating official wrote to his Commissioner of
Accounts, of all men, to conduct a raid on "anti-
American" history texts. That intrepid leader,
gathering a devoted band of propagandists—but
with no historians—set out "to preserve the
heroic old American history." They would listen
to nothing new, but preferred to lie back in in-

fantile delight in the arms of normalcy—the histories written for our grandfathers.

Nothing daunted these devoted patriots. They conducted what the valiant commissioner called "a 101 per cent. American investigation." If a sentence in its context would fail to shock the faithful, they took it out. One textbook writer, said the famous report, wrote that "Jefferson ought to have a halter about his neck," but the author had merely quoted that wish of Jefferson's enemies to show vividly how he was hated. One might as well assert that the Bible says "there is no God," neglecting to explain that that is merely what "the fool saith in his heart." This amazing report asserted that one author declared that Jefferson stole the Declaration of Independence, but what was really said was that the political ideas of that document were to be found in Locke, and other writers of the seventeenth century. By selecting and distorting items like these, and asserting them to reveal the tone of the book, the author was damned. There might be whole paragraphs of favourable things, stories of fine and heroic action which gave the real tone. These were ignored. If, by chance, the inquisitors found that the idea which displeased them in some text was after all the truth, vouched for even by Bancroft, their historical Aristotle, they solemnly rejected it, because truths revealed by research "tend to deaden the patriotic morale of school children." If, forsooth, the truth must be told, it must be "told optimistically." If the facts of history proved to be wholly opposed to his view, the stern censor threatened to go to the legislature and have them changed.

Finally there were horrifying omissions in some textbooks, one being a mention of Molly Pitcher; though, as all historians know, that good woman's reputation was so tarnished that a society of patriotic women in Philadelphia gave up the idea of a monument to her, and thanked their lucky stars when certain contemporary testimony was brought to their attention. After this ludicrous report was published at the expense of the patient tax-payers, one of the faithful henchmen of the newspaper king set out to spread its poison influence. This master of the mean art of confusing the vulgar mind fared forth to preach the twisted gospel to legislators, patriotic societies and school boards throughout the land. He talked, in his moderate way, of the "spirit of Benedict Arnold re-incarnated," of writers of "treason history" sending out "the poison gas of alien propaganda."

The seed being sown, the harvest was soon

ready to reap. Nobody took the pains to read the textbooks themselves, but the garbled versions were accepted as gospel truth. From every meeting, local or national, of patriotic societies came resolutions of protest. The Sons and Daughters of the Revolution, the Descendants of the Signers of the Declaration of Independence, the Spanish War Veterans, the American Legion, even the New Jersey Council of the Junior Order of the United Mechanics, and many others joined the chorus. All were convinced of the great danger of absorbing historical ideas not familiar to our parents. A learned judge, whom the United States Senate lately refused to appoint on President Coolidge's nomination to a federal judgeship, illustrated his judicial mind and his fitness to be, as he then was, President General of the National Society of the Sons of the American Revolution, by a vigorous assault upon all the best and most scholarly textbooks. The better the book, the more he hated it. "I want our school children," he cried, "taught that our forefathers were right, and the British were wrong.... The chief purpose to be subserved in teaching American history is the inculcation of patriotism." Oh! most wise and upright judge!

When this work had progressed far enough, the

politicians awoke to the opportunity to save the country. They drew up laws against all texts that "ignored, omitted, discounted, belittled, falsified, misrepresented, distorted, doubted or denied" the deeds—meaning, of course, the *traditional* deeds—of American patriots. Some of these bills were actually enacted. It was soon noted that it was not some sacred, one-sided tradition about the war with Spain or Mexico concerning which the facts must not be "falsified." Only the traditions about the two wars with Great Britain were protected by the sacred law of immutability. Moreover, some ungracious persons suggested that the constituents of the politicians, who pressed these bills the hardest, were more or less recent immigrants from the land where the shamrock grows, or from that of a late enemy country, whose war psychology was not yet dissipated. Can it be that the real trouble with the textbooks is that they are *not* anti-British, but *are* impartial? Why cannot the ordinary process of fair-minded criticism be applied to wars between Britain and America, as to wars between Prussia and France, Rome and Carthage? Why should an angel with a flaming sword stand before the gates of truth about the American Revolution, that our cherished off-spring may not enter and eat the fruit of the garden?

If patriotism and nationalism are to be taught by uncritical ancestor-worship, how are the future generations to get that solace for the disappointments in contemporary politics which comes from the discovery in critical histories that things used to be so much worse than they are now? One of the great rewards of the study of history is the preservation of our optimism, so often deadened by watching the pageant of present politics. If we are to have perfect ancestors, as in that so-called "American Legion History," which came as a climax to all this frantic effort to save American innocence, will not all the bombastic eulogy and maudlin sentimentality about "our virtues" and "our superiority" to other nations cause "our" next generation to behave like an insufferable cad toward the rest of the world? It is far better for the youth to learn that no "Kultur" is exclusive. It develops the aesthetic nature to live and think like the Greeks. It is ennobling to act like the Romans. It is sweet to enjoy the individual liberty of the English. It feeds the national pride to be as efficient as the Germans. It is a privilege and a glory to be an American.

But we need not fear the might of these Philistines, who would reject the truth and embrace propaganda. The facts of history will not budge.

24

One cannot change the events of history by resolutions of patriotic societies, nor yet by laws passed by sapient Solons—any more than one can change the eternal laws of Nature, as was attempted by that state legislature which tried to enact that hereafter the value of Pi should be an even 3 and not that bothersome 3·1416. Not Hearst, nor Hylan, nor Hirshfield, that aspirated trinity, can prevent the truth being taught at all the great universities to the present and the future teachers of history who have and will go out like a great army to teach what is true, regardless of what expurgated textbooks may be placed in their hands. Our King Canutes will soon be catching up their royal robes and flying ignominiously before the rising tide of truthful history.

Yet even if victory does finally "perch on the banners of the Burgundians," as the pompous old historian put it, is it not too bad that after all the toil in the musty archives and among forgotten books, the historian, after discovering the truth, must go out into the market place and fight for it? Perhaps he would do well to ignore the noisy *bandarlog*. I remember awakening one night in a sleeping car, of which I was the lone occupant, in the midst of an Indian jungle. Looking out of the window, I was alarmed to find no human habitation in sight, and the only sounds the cries of jackals and hyenas, and my imagination conjured up royal Bengal tigers, who might be very fond of the tender flesh of a professor. At first I was in a sad state of mind, but I reflected that this car was very likely left every night to be picked up by the Calcutta express. Finally I closed the window to a less space than I fancied necessary for the passage of Bengal tigers, and went back to sleep. When next I woke, my car was part of a noisy train, and we were rolling on to our destination. Perhaps that is the proper procedure in this hour when scholars view with alarm the yelps and howls of the jungle pack gathered about their sanctums of research. That conduct doubtless would be the part of wisdom, but historians could be more sure that their cause of truth would triumph, if they could feel that the best educated American citizens would keep abreast of the results of historical research, and join battle to preserve its conquests.

We of to-day have passed through the greatest crisis of human history. We are in a new world. There should be a striking increase of interest in human affairs. Our interest in the past and our sympathy should be the deeper because of those great events we have witnessed with a bleeding or rejoicing heart. We shall best understand any national problem if we have studied its roots in the past. History may be called the study by which the present age tries to understand itself by tracing its origins from the past. Citizens of a democracy owe that duty to the commonweal. A profound student of republican institutions has said, "The greater the number of people in a state who take trouble to form opinions of their own on public affairs.... the more wholesome the complexion of public opinion will be." Not only, as old Selden wrote, may the study of history "so accumulate years to us as if we had lived even from the beginning of time," but, as a wise contemporary has expressed it, "There is a provincialism in respect to time as narrowing as the provincialism of space, and one of the chief uses of history is to guard us from it."

The study of history has many intellectual rewards. It furnishes, declare its loving defenders, an antidote for the inexorable logic of mathematics and substitutes the habit of thinking in averages; accustoms the mind to deal with masses of people and centuries of time, develops a sense of the complexity of human affairs, and best of all cultivates the habit of toleration for many different views which may be held on nearly all complex questions. From its pursuit one learns easily and habitually to suspend judgment, and not to form unalterable opinions, based on a few haphazard facts. One gets the habit of analysis, the habit of synthesis, and above all a power of imagination. If one surrenders to the charms of Clio, and acquires those intellectual treasures, one will not suffer the agony of nervous solicitude for the honour of one's ancestors, nor join the benighted forces that strive for the permanent maintenance of the view that revolutionary British statesmen were monstrous tyrants, their soldiers depraved barbarians; but rather welcome truth whenever it appears, like the archangel of Mont St Michel, loving the heights.

Lecture II

THE RIVAL BRITISH AND AMERICAN
MERCHANTS IN THE REVOLUTION

The essayist, Addison, drew a very pleasing sketch of the British merchant in colonial days, who knits "mankind together in a mutual intercourse of good offices, distributes the gifts of Nature, finds work for the poor, adds wealth to the rich, and magnificence to the great." He "converts the tin of his own country into gold, and exchanges his wool for rubies. The Mahometans are clothed in our British manufacture, and the inhabitants of the frozen zone are warmed with the fleeces of our sheep." These were the merchant's graces, but because he pressed his benevolent services too vigorously at times, Benjamin Franklin addressed him with a sneer. "Nature," he wrote, "has put Bounds to your Abilities, tho' none to your Desires. Britain would if she could manufacture and trade for all the World; England for all Britain;—London for all England;—and every Londoner for all London." We may be sure that they were neither so idealistic nor so sordid as their admirers and their critics painted them. They had doubtless only the normal human selfishness, and were dominated as all men by the prevailing political and economic theories of their age.

One of the most universal of these ruling ideas was the mercantile theory. A famous Berlin economist holds that in its innermost kernel it was nothing but state-making and national economy-making, a spirit ruling all seventeenth and eighteenth century states, newly rising in Europe, and struggling to obtain and retain, each its own place, in the circle of nations; no statesman in that age was orthodox who did not measure the wealth of the nation in money, in gold or silver. Moreover, the followers of the true faith believed that all individual enterprise must be controlled by the state in the nation's interest: a merchant's trade was good or bad in so far as it filled or emptied this public treasure chest. A first principle of a nation's trade was that it should be so managed as to reduce the volume of foreign goods bought and therefore paid for with the nation's gold. Only second in importance was the tenet that a nation's industries should produce articles for export, which would absorb gold from neighbour nations, create a favourable balance of trade. By such ideas were British and all European merchants ruled, and all looked to their statesmen to act on these maxims.

Mercantilism, the policy of selfish nations, came to nothing else than an economic tussle among nations for wealth, for power, for prestige. It often ended in war, it always ended in jealousy and international bitterness. For colonies, the "children of nations," it meant subordination to the mother country, prostitution of their economic welfare to the interest of a selfish parent. If the "children" evaded laws to this end, the mercantilist sighed over their ungrateful natures, and looked about for means to bring them to obedience. As a result of the sway of this idea, colonies were conceived as occupied and cultivated territories, owned by the realm, useful only if they brought gain to the King and his people, resources for wars, prosperity to merchants. The lethargic imaginations of ministers could not picture them as living, political entities, with economic and social ambitions of their own, perhaps untaught in the sentiment of loyalty to an Empire. The government policy was, therefore, grown in the market place, rooted in the idea of gain to the homeland and its merchants. The colonies were "great farms of the public," the colonists were "tenants," to be treated kindly

31

unless they tried to get too independent, when they should be brought to book. British rulers wrapped in their own importance could never bear the thought of equality with provincials, never could understand their difficulties, never comprehend their grievances.

Dominated by the spirit and principles of mercantilism, the British Parliament, for over a century, enacted laws for colonial trade which were of three types. First there were acts of navigation which aimed to protect British shipowners against Dutch and French and Spanish—indeed, against all outside competition. Colonial shipowners did, however, share this protection, and shipbuilding so prospered in New England that a contemporary swore he never saw a more "amphibious population." Secondly there were acts of trade devised to maintain a monopoly of colonial commerce for English merchants. The colonial planter and the New England trader were forced to sell only to England, to buy only over British counters. George Washington of Virginia must sell his tobacco, Henry Laurens of South Carolina his indigo, rice and deer skins, to an English merchant. Both must buy furniture, hats and gloves from merchants of the same land. Either might have bought or sold to better profit in France or Holland, but in order that the duties on these goods might fill the King's exchequer, and the profits clink in British coffers, the law forbade. After 1760, some colonial exports paid in duties 60 per cent. of what they would bring in London markets.

A third class of laws, enacted to protect English interests, were those which aimed to secure English manufactures against the growth of rival industries in the colonies, and also to put in the hands of English manufacturers a monopoly of colonial markets. Even the friendly "Great Commoner" could declare that "if the Americans should manufacture a lock of wool or a horse shoe" he would "fill their ports with ships and their towns with troops." The effect of these three devices to put gold into English pockets was such that Edmund Burke could retort, to one who talked to him of colonial seas covered with ships and their rivers floating with commerce, "This is true; but it is with our ships that the seas are covered, and their rivers float with British commerce. The American merchants are our factors; all, in reality; most, even in name."

Therefore Navigation Acts—"guardians," "glorious bulwarks" of prosperity—made the colonies useful to England by extending her com-

merce. Colonies found favour not as new territories, new lands peopled with the English race,
reservoirs for the overflowing population of the
homeland, but as fertile fields whereon to grow
raw materials which otherwise must be bought in
France. The southern colonies, therefore, and the
West Indies, with tobacco, indigo, rice and sugar
to supplement England's natural products, were
regarded as far more useful to the "self-sufficing
empire" of the mercantilist than New England
which raised products of the same kind as the
home country. Although not wholly successful
in creating a new China and a new India on
American shores, the British Government did in
part escape dependence upon the Dutch and
Portuguese spice islands by getting from the
American mainland, or West India, pepper,
ginger, oranges, lemons, coffee and chocolate,
hardwoods, walnut, oak and mahogany, dye-
woods and indigo. Dependence on the northern
countries of Europe and other foreign lands was
lessened as a result of the multitudes of peltries
and furs, ranging from the marten to the buffalo,
from the beaver to the bear exported from nearly
every colony. Thence too came ship lumber, salt-
petre, and the by-products of the burning forests,
while the American fisheries greatly augmented

the supply of whale-oil, fins and spermaceti. But of all products sugar and tobacco were thought the most important mainstays of British prosperity.

The northern "bread colonies" made their chief contribution to imperial life in the foodstuffs and commodities sent to the West Indian and southern colonies. Colonies north of Maryland were not only considered less valuable to England, but they were actually her competitors and trade rivals, furnishing the fishermen of Newfoundland with cheaper shoes, lines, nets and food than could be bought in England. Moreover, their fishing ventures endangered her control of the fish trade with Europe. The chief offset to this danger was that in time of war the mercantilist valued the northern American colonies in terms of spruce and pine masts, bowsprits, yards and oaken lumber, wherewith to build the Royal Navy, to which the southern provinces added hemp and pitch and resin and tar. Nevertheless their value in the Empire seemed dubious, and advisers of Charles II urged him to hinder the growth of New England as much as possible.

The British trade regulations were criticized in America, (1) because of the duties, all too heavy, placed on colonial products laid down in British ports; (2) because colonial traders must carry "enumerated" commodities to England only—not to foreign ports; (3) because they must buy English plates and cutlery, English clothes—all needed manufactured goods—and were thus at the mercy of English monopolists—because in a word nearly all they bought and sold must pass over British counters and through British customs-houses to British profit and to colonial cost.

Colonial economists pointed out that, in addition to direct taxation by their own assemblies, the American provinces were contributing indirectly several hundred thousand pounds to the King's revenue yearly. It has been estimated that, in wages and profits and all, America added £2,000,000 to British income yearly. The British "interests," to use our modern phraseology, were being protected by British law while they exploited the common people of both America and England, but the American common people were more homogeneous, and far enough removed not to be easily subjected. The conditions of American life made the people more sensitive, more ready to resist, more hospitable to radical ideas of resistance. Their immediate escape was smuggling and illicit trade. In this direction lay trade freedom, independent commercial life. To this contempt for law were the colonists driven by the principles and acts of "mercantilists."

Some crabbed critics in our twentieth century go so far as to say that the mercantilist doctrine of self-sufficiency and exclusiveness still rules in the "land of the free" and "the home of the brave." They talk of high tariffs, and a belief in the virtues of isolation, and plans to exploit dependencies, as evidences of a similar spirit to that which ruled in Europe in the eighteenth century. They insinuate that government for the benefit of the "interests," that politicians who ask, "What have we to do with abroad," that a tendency to look upon trade as a form of warfare wherein all measures are fair, are all manifestations of a spirit like that of the hateful mercantilist. Those who measure prosperity by the excess of exports over imports are, say these gloomy American deans, little better than mercantilists or one of the wicked. Some dreamy philosophers talk of a coming age when trade policies at daggers drawn will pass away, and nations will seek mutual understanding, unselfish associations among themselves. The historian of course has nothing to do with such uncharitable reflections upon his age, nor with idle speculations about the future, but must pass on to reflective meditation, on the past.

Though our modern eyes find much to criticize in Britain's regulation of her colonies, yet politically the American provinces were far more free than those of Spain or France, and the colonies were not without advantages under the sway of Navigation Laws. Colonial staples were given a monopoly of the home market, colonial ships shared the favours enjoyed by English ships, and there were bounties to stimulate the raising certain products—indigo, hemp, naval stores, and even silk. A British historian says that the colonial merchants accepted "all enactments or monopolies working in their own favour, obeyed and observed none of the enactments restrictive of their own operations, and proceeded, as regards the merchants and manufacturers of Great Britain, very much on the principle of 'heads I win, tails you lose.'" Though rather ungentle and overstated, one cannot honestly say that it is untrue. Moreover, the British protective system worked pretty well at first as far as the colonies were concerned which had different interests, but the colonies of the north were too much like the homeland in natural conditions and economic character, were, in a word, not complementary but rivals.

Besides the economic advantages which eased the economic shackles borne by the colonists, one must recognize that in an age of real peril from powerful enemies, the trade of all the colonies was protected by the Royal Navy. All trade between England and America was harassed by many ills. There were hurricane seasons, wind and storm, villainous captains, leaky ships, wrecks, pirates, slow voyages, dishonest agents, wastage, shrinkage, war which raised rates of insurance, freight and prices, and caused embargoes. In the colonial ports there was all the carelessness of a frontier community about inspection, and as a result their products arrived in bad shape, tobacco black, sour and of poor quality, wheat weevily, flour ill-bolted, coarse and musty, lumber ill-seasoned, many things unsaleable. Most trade was a gamble, but it flourished nevertheless. Against all these ills which were not "acts of Providence" or freaks of Nature the British Government and the Royal Navy furnished most of what protection existed. But it was hard for the colonist to realize this guardianship. That fleet which warded the enemy from American shores, and kept supplies from the French army in Canada, and created what fear there was in the hearts of the pirates and privateers of that age, was not spectacular, and its long and weary vigils out at sea were easily forgotten. Its work was not done in the view of the colonists, rarely obviously performed for their good, and was not thought of as one of the obligations to England. It was only when it was too late that American sea-traders began to compute the value of Britannia's rule of the watery wastes of the earth, and to realize that the protection of their trade by the powerful British Empire was not to be sneered at in a world tense with commercial rivalry.

Though the principles of the mercantilists may seem wrong, it must be granted that the British policy based on it was remarkably successful, and appears at least to have put Great Britain to the very fore among nations fighting in the eighteenth century for sea power, trade and colonies. Later the French republic imitated it; Napoleon, too, paid it that sincere compliment. Moreover, it cannot be over-emphasized that the British commercial policy was not capricious, not born of a whim to tyrannize, nor a desire to meddle. It was based on principles ruling the administrative mind of all Europe, and the conviction that no colony was doing its duty as a subordinate and ancillary part of the Empire if it tried to act merely for its own interest, and thus changed that course of trade ordained by British law.

The reason that the British failed at last to solve

in time their great imperial problem was that their colonial government machine had no other object than the regulation of trade and commerce in the best interests of the home country. Parliament, busy with the momentous affairs of the kingdom, and later of the Empire, had little time to spare for all the masses of facts concerning colonial problems, which an assiduous Board of Trade huddled together for its inspection. The ministry saw nothing colonial with its own eyes, and what it learned indirectly concerned trade alone and how to make it profitable to the Crown.

Yet the historian may not attribute the American Revolution, as did Arthur Young, solely to the "baleful spirit of commerce, that wished to govern great nations on the maxims of the counter." Imperialism, and faulty plans to carry out its aims led the British rulers still further toward the abyss. When by 1750 there were two millions of people in the English colonies—multiplying like their own rattlesnakes, as the sweet spirited Dr Johnson expressed it—they began to attract attention as a fine lot of consumers, a good public to sell to, as well as to raise products needed in England. With that dawning appreciation a new philosophy as to the uses of colonies began to kindle in the administrative mind. It was appreciation of this new theory which made William Pitt wonder which he should be "hanged for not keeping," Canada or Guadeloupe, when the Seven Years' War should end. He saw, among the first to see, that a colony might increase the strength of England by giving room where English seed might multiply, where market places might rise for English goods. By the time rebellion impended in America one-sixth to one-third of all trade carried on by English merchants was with the colonies, an enormous increase since 1700. This was a change that might well stir the imaginations of even duller men than sat in the British Parliament.

It is hard to realize that a British Empire, "England with all her daughter lands about her," a state scattered over the seven seas, and ruled from Westminster, was hardly dreamed of in the early eighteenth century. As late as 1763 there was little thought of opening up new territory where English seed might be planted, and in time a fine crop of Englishmen might grow, furnishing a new market for British manufacturers. Colonies must "pay as they go." But the taking of Canada and the vast areas beyond the Alleghanies meant that a new policy prevailed. Regions had been incorporated in the Empire which could not pay for their "keep" for years to come. It was the effort to pay these "imperial" expenses which led Parliament on and on to a disruption of the Empire.

With Pitt's decision to take Canada the old-fashioned mercantilist, of course, had no patience. Hence Pitt's scorn of the "little, paltry, peddling fellows, vendors of twopenny wares and falsehoods, who under the idea of trade sell everything in their power—honour, truth, conscience." Not to see the golden vision of empire was, in the "Great Commoner's" mind, to weigh affairs of state in the scales of trade. But his scorn was of no avail. Mercantilists, valuing colonies only for their trade, could not harbour the thought of a colony that did not pay its way, of one that was supported for the greater glory of a prince and his empire of hungry subjects. Those ministers, therefore, who inherited the consequences of Pitt's decision must so mould their plans of empire as not to shock too severely the conservatives still thinking the old thoughts, tethered to the rock of mercantilism.

In the newly acquired areas beyond the Alleghanies there were imperial problems and clashing interests. The fur traders would intrigue to have it left as wild as possible, the land companies would scheme to get it settled and cleared as fast as might be; the friends of the Redman would strive to have his interests protected against the unscrupulous fur trader and the on-pressing settler. In the new region, also, imperial interests would vie with those of individual colonies having land claims. Lord Shelburne's carefully devised plan to meet all these problems was made but not applied, when he was forced from office, and the Grenville-Bedford faction, succeeding to power, set out to administer what they ill understood, and began the wrecking of the Empire. To finance the expense of an army intended to enforce the regulations of the back-country they entered upon a series of colonial measures which invoked revolution. It had been Shelburne's intention not to tax the colonies at first for the support of the army, but Grenville had no such scruples, and though the British merchant might have been ready to submit to a greater load of taxes at home, expecting the land-holding class to bear it, Parliament, dominated by landowners, preferred to load the colonies with the cost of opening up the western lands. Grenville's first attempt to raise a revenue, therefore, was an effort securely to fasten the strait-jacket of trade upon the colonial victim. The old Molasses Act (1733), about to expire, had been devised to force New England distillers and sellers of rum to buy their molasses and sugar and rum from British sugar planters, and to keep them out of the Spanish and French West Indies. Class legislation, colonists called it, for a few "pampered Creolians," at the expense of two million American subjects. Smuggling, on such a scale as to make illicit trade the rule and not the exception, had made the revenue law a dead letter, defraying not a quarter of the cost of collecting. Now, 1764, Grenville got a re-enactment of the old act, slightly modified, and the molasses duty reduced to lessen the profits of smuggling. He then increased the force of revenue officers, sent all the holders of sinecures to their posts in the customs-houses of America, increased the war-vessels on guard along the sea-board, and made legal the use of general writs so that customs officers could go into any American house wherein they believed there were smuggled goods. The barriers placed upon illegal trade were perhaps the greatest offence, for without the proceeds of the illicit trade with the French and Spanish islands, the northern merchants at least did not see how they were to get the gold and silver or bills of exchange with which to pay their English creditors.

The trade restrictions by the British Government had been endured in the past because they had been nullified. The rapidly growing northern colonies would accept no secondary place in the British Empire and smuggled where they could not trade freely. Smuggling was not in colonial parlance a polite name by which to call the evasions of the trade laws; men preferred to call it a defiance of British sovereignty. If the fortune of a colonial family was swollen by illicit trade, extending even to a treasonable commerce with the French enemy in Canada during the Seven Years' War, it was no blot on the scutcheon. Little smugglers only envied the volume of the smuggling enterprises of John Hancock and other great merchants. Smuggling was only an ornament of their respectability. No blush of shame came to the patriotic cheeks of the members of the first Continental Congress when one of them declared without fear of contradiction, "Many gentlemen in this room know how to bring in goods, sugars and others, without paying duties." Smuggling was not in the bright lexicon of American crimes. In order to free a neighbour and fellow smuggler, a colonial jury had been known to find that soap and candles were food-stuffs, and therefore "provisions" which might under the law be freely imported. The New England coast with its creeks, coves and rocky inlets seemed designed by Nature to aid the trade of a smuggler. James Otis defied the king of England in person, at the head of 20,000 men camped on Boston Common and all his navy on the coast, to execute the trade laws. His Majesty's collectors of customs found casks of wine and boxes of fruit lying in the shrubbery of their gardens, and other influential persons, as in Kipling's famous verses on smuggling in England, found a bit of lace for madam and "baccy for the parson, brandy for the clerk." They all knew that the bounties of Providence would continue if they shut their eyes when illegal cargoes of wine and fruit were being landed at the wharves. One hundred and fifty years before the Volstead Act Americans were training for the dry age that was to come. So successful were they that in Rhode Island alone 11,500 out of 14,000 hogsheads of molasses imported yearly, most of which was made into rum, were smuggled from the French and Spanish West Indies. In New England alone the cunning of the smugglers cost the British treasury probably £100,000 each year.

John Adams confessed, years after the Revolution, that molasses was an essential ingredient in American independence. The stopping of most of the illicit trade in that commodity took away the

47

balance in gold and silver with which colonial merchants satisfied those British creditors who had supplied them with glass and locks and hinges and manufactured finery. A flame of protest swept the affected colonies. Though it seems to have been imperialism, not mercantilism, which was the most important immediate cause of rebellion and war, yet it must be remembered that the laws founded on mercantile theories had not been obeyed, and the imperialists' efforts to enforce them, to stop smuggling and illicit trade, fired the first resentment of American merchants.

When Grenville's legislation of 1764 injured the merchants of Philadelphia, Boston and New York, nothing was more to be expected than their effort to arouse the colonial public to protest against this blow at American prosperity. Yet resentment of the colonial merchants towards the Sugar Act might easily have been mollified. Parliament was fairly open-minded to trade grievances; but the Stamp Act, a direct tax, threatening to drain the little ready money they had, the first attempt to make the colonies pay directly for the new imperialism, and hitting hardest the merchants, printers and lawyers, was not so easily adjusted. Both acts would drain off the silver and gold with which colonial merchants hoped to meet their trade balances. The troubles of the great merchants were of course passed on to the man in the street, the grocer and baker, the small farmer and shop-keeper—and these joined the cries of wrath against the oppressor.

The rage of the colonial merchants soon reacted upon the British merchants, already distressed by hard times at home, scarcity and high cost of goods, rising wages, numerous business failures. They opposed, therefore, laws which distressed their American customers, and let the colonists know that they were bringing pressure high and low to get a repeal of the hateful acts. In Parliament the country squires, the lords of manors, the wealthy bourgeoisie did not always see eye to eye with the rich city merchants as to where the incidence of taxation should rest, whether on broad acres or on the nation's trade. In this instance the latter were more than usually successful. Aided by non-consumption and non-importation acts in America, the British merchants secured Parliament's attention, and got the act repealed, as contrary to the true principles of commerce, against the mercantile theory. It was this, rather than the colonial outcry against the illegal encroachments of the Crown, which brought about Parliament's retreat.

Two years later the Townshend Acts, again hampering trade and inspired by the old desire of raising revenue for imperial purposes, kept on the anvil the old question of subordination of colonial to English prosperity. Once more there was in America non-importation, a flame moving slowly southward and growing less alarming as it receded from its source. Again the merchants entered into alliance with more radical groups, farmers, small tradesmen and ambitious young lawyers with a gift for harangue, who pressed resistance to extremes, which led to the sending of two regiments of British soldiers to Boston, and the ill-omened "Boston Massacre." Resolves, pamphlets, acts of violence and commercial boycotts, which again alarmed the British merchants, finally convinced even Lord North that the obnoxious acts were costing the King more than they brought to his treasury, were wrong in commercial principle, and must in part at least be repealed. Retaining one tax, that on tea, "to keep up the right," Parliament repealed the duties and the storm seemed over.

But keeping "the yoke about the neck of the Americans" to preserve the dignity of England proved a costly bit of vanity. The American merchants paid little attention at first to the yoke, because the great ones at least had grown weary of stirring the masses, who then did rash things and too easily got out of hand. The zeal for non-importation lagged, the well-to-do could get smuggled tea, and the radicals grew anxious about the peaceful temper of their neighbours.

When, however, in 1773 the East India Company was on the verge of bankruptcy—a vast surplus stock on its hands—Parliament blindly granted it what came to a monopoly of the tea trade with America. It could select its own agents to sell tea in the colonies and these could under-sell, through the favours of the act, not only the regular tea merchants, but even the smugglers of Dutch tea. Like the Atlantic and Pacific Company of to-day, it cut out the middleman's profits, and sold direct to the consumer. Still there might have been no trouble, had the company chosen as its American agents the merchants there who had been accustomed to handle the London tea trade. Instead it was merchants who had lately opposed non-importation agreements who were selected. Besides the actual tea monopoly the injured merchants conjured up the possibility of one that would extend to spices, silks, drugs, every foreign commodity in which they dealt. Ruin stared them in the face. Yet they would probably have opposed the danger with legal means, but that Samuel Adams seized upon their new grievance as an opportunity to push matters to the extreme, and blew up such a storm as ended in spreading the cargoes of the tea ships over the waters of Boston Harbour, making tea for all the cod-fish on the banks of Newfoundland, as a gleeful Whig wrote. The tea once landed would have been sold, the radicals feared, and the tea-party was necessary, because Boston patriotism could not be trusted to resist the charms of the tea leaf. The merchants had not been able to control the situation as in 1766 and 1770, and, after the mischief had been done, sixty-three in Boston signed a protest in which they repented the destruction of property, and would have had Boston pay the bill for its party. Not so John Adams, however, who drew heavily on his verbal resources to express his ad-miration. The "dignity," "majesty," "sublimity" of the affair, caused him to view it as an epoch in human history. Benjamin Franklin disapproved and hoped for "voluntary reparation." Most of America's friends in England regretted the "tur-bulent and unwarrantable" act.

On the whole the early results in America seemed a set-back to radical power, so that great was the delight of the "Saviours of the People" when Lord North changed the whole character of the controversy from one over trade regulation, and the right to tax unrepresented people, to a question of the political right of the British Parliament to punish the people of Boston by the ruin of their trade and the complete change of their government. On the enactment of the "Five Intolerable Acts" Franklin commented, "Divine Providence first infatuates the power it designs to ruin," and Colonel Barré warned the British nation, "Let the banners of rebellion be once spread in America, and you are an undone people."

The most momentous result in America of coercive measures was the assembling of the First Continental Congress. Of its measures the one which most nearly touched the American merchants was the "Continental Association" binding all supporters of the Congress not to use or import British goods with few exceptions, and, after a year, to export nothing thither unless American rights had all been granted. Local Whig committees everywhere were to blacklist all who refused to follow these injunctions. All this was far from welcome to the great merchant who foresaw a cessation of profits for months to come. The work of the First Continental Congress was, therefore, a defeat of the merchant power in America and of all who wished moderation. Soon every colonial merchant who feared anarchy, and was concerned for the safety of extensive property interests, was driven to Loyalism. The merchant dressed in London styles, whose mansion walls were rich with ancestral faces done in oil, and whose world-wide trade throve under imperial protection, grew wary of his late tools, the leaders of riots, the "Jack Cades" who roared "liberty" in a tavern, and demanded, as a reward for his support of the "rights of man," a right to vote and to hold office. Law and order began to have greater attractions than "liberty," as interpreted by the "lower orders of mankind." The privileged classes began to face the issue of whether they could maintain their privileges against ministerial encroachment from above without losing them by popular encroachment from below. Merchants asked each other, Are we more in danger from the oppression of laws made in London or from the insurgence of radicals from the wharves and back streets of Boston? Yet it was true of many that attachment to country right or wrong, a conviction that British policy endangered all rights and liberties, or perhaps mere self-interest, the dominant desire to save one's skin, forced them to the radical side, either as hearty or moderate Whigs.

Possibly many of the latter were influenced by what Jonathan Boucher called an "other circumstance favourable to a revolt in America, that of the immense debt, owing by the colonists to the merchants of Great Britain." From the middle of the eighteenth century on, America became more and more to be the greatest of the consumers of British goods. Scotch and British merchants ran a mad race for this growing trade even though it depended on long term credits in the colonies or was founded on capital borrowed in the British Isles. Speculation, inflation of credit went so far just on the eve of the Revolution that American debtors despaired of ever paying the staggering sums, and the British merchants were full of forebodings. Little gold, and inadequate surplus of staple products, made payments difficult—possible even in part because of the illegal trade carried on with the French and Spanish West Indies. All this was made worse because the British trader, as the eighteenth century wore on, became less interested in receiving colonial raw materials, especially those of the north, heavy and hard to sell, and wanted money instead. As a result bills of exchange mounted higher and higher, the burdens of credit became heavier and heavier until we marvel at the risks the British merchants dared to take. Yet an orgy of trade after 1770 sent up American debts to some £3,000,000, reaching £5,000,000 before war began. An illusory prosperity based on paper money issues and swollen credits deceived nearly all. In northern towns and on southern plantations standards of living rose, new tastes created demands for more varied and luxurious manufactured goods, almost unlimited credit made indulgence easy, and, with every trade expansion, more British merchants, more English manufacturing towns became bound to American interests. It is these facts which account for their pleading with Parliament to repeal obnoxious acts. Just before the war broke out almost every planter or store-keeper in the south was in debt to British merchants—Virginia to the amount of nearly £2,500,000—and confidence in ultimate payment was oozing away. It would be unwise to emphasize this matter of debts as a cause of revolution, but the facts ought to be presented.

Except for this weighty argument of their debts, the merchants, charmed with the golden benefits of protection by the British sea power and empire, were not allured either early or late by the vision of independence. Better treatment within the Empire, not separation from it, was their slogan, as long as they could make it heard. Republican

sentiments and a levelling philosophy, voiced by
noisy mass meetings and destructive mobs, were
alarming, not pleasing to them.

After the "Boston Tea Party" and the "Five
Intolerable Acts" it is hard to see how the quarrel
could have stopped short of war, given the
mentality of the leaders on both sides. There
seemed left no grounds of mutual understanding.
If American merchants proposed a concession of
commercial advantages, they were called enemies
of liberty, their motives unpatriotic and mercenary.
The liberty they demanded was called rebellion.
A supporter of the king declared that "Britain,
like the pelican, had fed her young with her blood;
grown strong, they rose up to prey upon her
vitals." Harrington had wondered long ago why
princes liked to be exhausted in that way.

If King George proposed any limits upon
colonial self-control, or based his claim on law or
royal prerogative, he heard in reply the bitter cry
of "tyranny," "despotism." What the colonial
leaders called the unchanging human conceptions
of what was right and what was wrong were
summoned to justify American resistance to "op-
pressive" laws of Parliament. Even the English
merchants, when called to the aid of their good
customers in America by the startling vision of

closing markets, found their petitions in vain, the Government, grim and determined, bent on rule or ruin. When petitions rained upon Parliament from Belfast, Birmingham, Glasgow, Leeds and Manchester, presaging ruin if America were not conciliated, North refused to let America rebel and slip behind creditors for protection. Moreover, the fact that Americans had of late dwelt more upon their political and less upon their economic rights and upon the evil commercial consequences of the British laws, decreased the influence of the mercantile class in Parliament, until by 1775 that class seemed to have lost all its power to move the British legislature.

Thus the English merchant, for whose supposed interests and those of the kingdom's exchequer the mercantilist laws had been enacted, came at last to be ignored by the Government, controlled by the great families, the landowners, the squires, bent on realizing an imperial idea fated to stir rebellion in America. Defoe had declared that "trade is so far from being inconsistent with a gentleman that in short, trade in England makes a gentleman; for after a generation or two, the tradesmen's children, or at least their grandchildren, come to be as good gentlemen, statesmen, parliament-men, privy-councillors, judges, bishops as those of the highest families." Yet in spite of this dictum there were few mere merchants in Parliament and their cries were unheard when the ruling class—gentlemen, bishops and noblemen, to use Defoe's description—intrenched in the government offices and in the Parliament, set out to rule or ruin. If this privileged class, unfriendly to reform, firm in the seat of political power, scorned the pleas of the merchant interests in England, it was not strange that they were deaf to the American merchants' outcries sounding feebly across the vast spaces of the ocean. The imperial plan, chosen with perfectly good intent on the part of the British Government, looked to the Americans like a plot to establish tyranny, yet, to the official eyes, with only the dim light which the past experience of mankind then offered, the concessions, which might have forestalled the Revolution, would have taken away all the value of the colonies to Britain, and endangered the prosperity of the Empire. Americans, free to elect their own rulers, rid of all Parliamentary authority, making their own rules of trade, what value were they to Great Britain? Could an empire violate the ten commandments of mercantilism and survive? The answer of Lord North was, No! and the result was the American Revolution.

Lecture III

THE ANGLICAN CHURCH
AND THE DISSENTERS IN THE
AMERICAN REVOLUTION

Not six months before that fatal shot on Lexington Green the royal Governor of North Carolina wrote to the Earl of Dartmouth that to the reproach of Christian people on both sides "distinctions and animosities have immemorially prevailed in this Country between the people of the established Church and the Presbyterians on the score of the difference of their unessential modes of Church Government; and the same spirit of division has entered into or been transferred to most of their concernments." At present, he added, "there is no less apparent schism between their Politics than in matters appertaining to religion." While "Loyalty, Moderation and respect to Government seem to distinguish the generality of the members of the Church of England," whose principles, indeed, he found more congenial with the British form of government, "I am sincerely sorry to find that they are by no means the characters of the Presbyterians at large." In fact, he added, "the people of this denomination in general throughout the continent are not of the principles of the Church of Scotland, but like the people of New England, more of the leaven of the Independents, who according to English story have been ever unfriendly to the Monarchical Government." The same state of tension between Anglican and Dissenter was noticed five years earlier in Rhode Island where a Loyalist found the "face of public affairs" very melancholy, "altar against altar in the Church, and such open, bold attacks upon the State" as English annals had not shown since the days of King Charles I. In the middle colonies also, Joseph Galloway, most notable of all Loyalists, found the disaffection confined to two sets of dissenters, Presbyterians and Congregationalists; while the people of the Established Church were warmly attached to the British Government. A thousand attestations of this generalization exist in the records of the Revolution. Its cause and results are worthy of consideration.

The early migrations to America had been largely due to the political and religious conflicts of the age. English Kings, in their zeal to people the colonies, had planted the seeds of revolution, tempted the radicals and dissenters to migrate to

America. Men who became the fathers of New England, had insisted upon going to Heaven in their own way, and bred a political dislike of all rulers who tried to drive them along the Episcopalian's road to salvation. To "plant churches by power," to "compel religion" was wrong in their way of thinking. They denied the right of King or Parliament to force them by laws and penalties to submit to any ecclesiastical forms. In reply the British Government shut to the Puritans or Separatists in England every gate to public activity in Church or State, barred them by Courts of High Commission, the Star Chamber and the Tower. When thus it made Dissenters so unhappy that they fled to America, the Government seems merely to have put off for one hundred and fifty years, and removed to another shore, the struggle between defenders of the Established Church on one side and their opponents, the radicals, antagonistic to Church and secular government.

When the Puritan vanguard was safe in New England, Cotton Mather, one of their spiritual leaders, wrote, "Let all mankind know that we came into the wilderness, because we would worship God without that Episcopacy, that common prayer, and those unwarrantable ceremonies, with which the land of our forefathers' sepulchres has been defiled." And the reverend Increase Mather added, "There never was a generation that did so perfectly shake off the dust of Babylon, both as to ecclesiastical and civil constitution, as the first generation of Christians that came into this land for the gospel's sake." There, indeed, they were free "from the iron yokes of wolfish bishops," and could forget titles—even that of "His Majesty" —and their only fear was of the "high displeasure of the King of Kings." Little wonder that King James thought Presbyterianism agreed as well with monarchy "as God and the Devil," and that, on the eve of the American Revolution, Loyalists asserted that all English Kings had been worried by Presbyterian rebellions, that "Presbyterianism and rebellion were twin sisters." People of that sect "are and have always been," declared a friend of George III, "a set of uneasy, discontented and innovating people." Well might they be, for, as has been truly said, Latimer was their preacher, Milton their poet, Bunyan their solemn romancer, Locke and Sydney their political thinkers, and Hampden and Pym their statesmen.

Not only did the Congregationalist and the Presbyterian hold principles dangerous to kingship and an established church, but his whole outlook on life was different from that of the conventional Anglican churchman. The latter, travelling in the colonies and mingling with dissenters, was amazed at the spiritual gloom that pervaded life. He found that one of the "best-sellers" in the literary world was Dent's *Plain Man's Pathway to Heaven, wherein every man may clearly see whether he shall be saved or damned*. Wigglesworth's *Day of Doom*, which described the damnation of the non-elect babes for the guilt of Adam's sin and conceded to them merely "the easiest room in hell," was another favourite with Dissenters. This book which pictured Christ as now a "Moloch" now a "New England Dogberry" was described in Boston papers as "those divine poems." The most famous preachers dwelt on such themes in their sermons. The Puritan mind, pleased with the thought of that "fiery deluge, fed with ever burning sulphur unconsumed," frowned upon "the smooth divine unused to wound the sinner's heart with Hell's alarming sound." The Anglican traveller found his dissenting American host horrified to learn that a neighbour, when lately in London, had learned to play cards, and had visited Kew on Sunday, or, even worse, had scandalized all God-fearing men by going to hear *Hamlet* and *Othello*. Even an Episcopalian governor could not cause a maypole to be set up in Puritan

Massachusetts without being amazed at a blaze of indignation which followed. The spruce and laurel with which he sought to give a holiday air to Government House at Christmas time he found was forbidden by law. It were better, like the pious Sewall, to pass the day arranging the coffins in the family vault, "an awful but pleasing diversion."

The very contrast between the service in a colonial Episcopalian Church and that in any of the Dissenting churches was marked. "The service of the English Church appeared to me," wrote Chastellux, "a sort of opera, as well for the music as the decorations: a handsome pulpit placed before a handsome organ; a handsome minister in that pulpit, reading, speaking and singing with a grace entirely theatrical, a number of young women answering melodiously from the pit and boxes, a soft and gentle vocal music with excellent sonatas, playing alternately on the organ; all this compared to the Quakers, the Anabaptists, the Presbyterians appeared to me rather a little paradise itself, than as the road to it." But such a church was "Egypt's Babylon" in Dissenters' eyes.

Their spiritual characters standing in so great contrast, there was bound to be friction wherever

Anglican and Dissenter came in contact. It was the custom of the British Government to fill all Colonial offices with "ruffle-shirted Episcopalians," and in the northern colonies, where Dissenters were dominant, and attended their own churches, officials, attending Anglican churches, missed the social contact which might have given them a better understanding and sympathy with the people whom they ruled. Only exceptionally was there a Dr Jekyll and Mr Hyde, like Governor Dudley, who went to King's Chapel to impress the Government with his Anglican zeal, and at the same time said with a wink to his Massachusetts friends that at heart he was still a Congregationalist. As a rule, officials were zealous in behalf of the Church, and as their sectarian prejudices became hateful, their governing functions became the more odious.

It was the duty of every governor to see that the Book of Common Prayer was read and the "Blessed Sacrament" administered each Sunday and Holy Day—an offence in itself to the bigoted Dissenter. Andros tried in the very sanctuary of Puritanism to place marriages solely in the hands of the Anglican clergy. All dissenting sects in America were alarmed by the activity of the Bishop of London in getting political plums for those who would be useful allies of the Anglican Church in the colonies. No schoolmaster could go thither without a licence from him; no minister to any benefice there without his certificate. William Penn's charter compelled him to admit to his asylum for Quakers ministers appointed by the Lord Bishop, if a certain number of colonists requested. Indeed, the Bishop of London was called into consultation with the Board of Trade as to all laws affecting the interests of Churchmen in America, and very often his will prevailed over that of Colonial Dissenters, even to the disallowance of acts dear to their hearts. Laws for the disposal of parish property, reducing the salaries of Anglican ministers, or providing penalties for their immoral conduct were annulled by royal veto on advice from the Bishop, greatly to the disgust of the Dissenters. True, the power of the Board and the Bishop was used at times to enforce toleration for persecuted sects, but that was no less offensive to Dissenters, bent on securing the hegemony of Puritan churches. All plans to bring every colonial government directly under control of the Crown were backed with ardour by the Anglican Church. Having once driven the Dissenters out of England, and for a time neglected them, the Church awoke to the importance of this mighty province in the Empire, and set about to tear down the power of the Puritan in New England, the Quaker in Pennsylvania, and to regain this lost opportunity for ecclesiastical expansion.

One of the endeavours to this end, to which the British Government never held out a helping hand, was the establishing an Anglican Episcopate in America. There was much to be said for bringing Mahomet to the mountain, a bishop to America. Otherwise every colonial candidate for ordination must face a voyage to England and back, six thousand miles in a sailing vessel. If he were not drowned going over he might drown coming back, and few were "moved by the Holy Ghost," as Mayhew sneered, to face the danger or expense. As a result the Anglican clergy in America were often such as had failed in England, shepherds to whom their flocks looked up and were not fed. Though there were differences of opinion it was believed that they drank harder than they prayed, were more faithful to card-playing than to their congregations, and were better connoisseurs of fighting cocks than of souls. As to the latter, perhaps they agreed with Sir Edward Seymour, "Souls, sir, damn your souls. Make tobacco," for their salaries were paid in that commodity. To remedy this evil either the Society for the Propagation of the Gospel in Foreign Parts or the Bishop of London pressed a plan from time to time to found an American Episcopate.

Against this pious effort Dissenters in America arose in fierce protest, especially in the two decades just before the Revolution. They would have none of the "pomp, grandeur, luxury and regalia of an American Lambeth," no "Apostolical monarch," nor "right reverend and holy tyrants." Puritan ministers warned their flocks against "imperious bishops" who "love to lord it over God's heritage." They pictured Presbyterianism being rooted out or consumed by the "flames of Episcopacy." New England's spirit of parsimony was enkindled by talk of "pontifical revenues," of tithes to support a bishop. Above all, emphasis was laid on the fact that if done, it must be by an act of Parliament, and that if it could create a bishop it could tax. Though the British ministry seems never to have considered the Anglican project seriously, they were suspected of doing so, and the fear in the American mind became one of the causes of alienation.

Though nearly all Dissenters north of Maryland opposed the plan of an American Episcopate while Episcopalians embraced it, yet in the south opinion did not divide on the same lines. The Virginian laity already had state control of the Episcopalian Church of which most of the planters were members, and they wanted no intrusion by the British Government. Only a part even of the clergy favoured the creation of an American bishop, and they, it was said, influenced by the ambition for a pair of lawn sleeves. The truth seems to be that the Virginian Episcopalians were alienated from a Church buttressed by the British Government, not taking the union of Church and the English State over-seriously, willing to have Virginia taxed to support *their* church, but not the Anglican Church. The famous "Parson's Cause," in which the Bishop of London took the side of the Crown, had led many to resent any effort of the British Government to protect its spiritual shepherds in America.

Besides this special assault of the Dissenting clergy upon the Anglican Church, there was, during the whole colonial period, a never-ceasing antagonism to all church doctrines which upheld the divine right of kings, submission and obedience to them. John Adams, in his most thumping manner, declared that the New England Puritans had "an utter contempt for all that dark ribaldry of hereditary, indefeasible right—the Lord's anointed—and the divine miraculous original of government, with which priesthood had enveloped the feudal monarch and whence they had deduced the most mischievous of all doctrines, that of passive obedience and non-resistance." Immoderate as Adams was, he only related the historic truth that Presbyterian and Congregationalist ministers had long preached the doctrines of political liberty taught by Sidney, Milton, Locke and Hoadly in the seventeenth century. As the progeny of the rebel Puritans of Cromwell's time, "those hypocritical fanatics who brought the best of princes to the block," they felt obliged to defend the doctrines of political liberty, which had moved their ancestors, and they found a great arsenal of bookish weapons in the writings of Locke and Milton. They did not always incite to rebellion, or even preach discontent, but they stated to their congregations the theories of Locke, discussed the origin, nature and end of government, the rights of man, the axiom that it was the people's right to choose their own rulers and fix the bounds of their authority. As early as 1630 a New England preacher taught his flock that "the choice of public magistrates belongs unto the people by God's own allowance. They who have the power to appoint officers and magistrates, it is in their power also to set the bounds and limitations of the power and place into which they call them." Since the pulpit then and for generations after was, in New England at least, the most direct and effective way of reaching the masses, such ideas grew apace in the minds of the people.

On the subject of the right of people to rise even against their king "to break the yoke of tyranny," two very antagonistic doctrines came from Anglican and Dissenting pulpits in America. Young Anglican clergy, fresh from Oxford, taught that "submission and obedience, clear, absolute and without exception" was "the badge and character of the Church of England." A common theme of their sermons was the duty of the people to pray for and praise their rulers, and a favourite text among them was, "Let every soul be subject unto the higher powers, for there is no power but of God; the powers that be are ordained of God; whosoever therefore resisteth the power, resisteth the ordinance of God, and they that resist shall receive to themselves damnation." On the anniversary of Charles I's "martyrdom" the clergy were compelled to read the Oxford homily or preach against disobedience or wilful rebellion.

In resistance to all this American "Roundheads" thundered. Jonathan Mayhew, spiritual leader of the American Revolution, argued (1750) the right of people to free themselves from inglorious servitude and ruin. "It is upon this principle that many royal oppressors have been driven...into banishment, and many slain by the hands of their subjects....(that) Tarquin was expelled from Rome, and Julius Caesar...cut off in the Senate House...that Charles I was beheaded before his own banqueting house;...that King James II was made to fly that country which he had aimed at enslaving." When Patrick Henry uttered like thoughts a few years later some Anglican auditors greeted them with cries of "treason."

On the subject of Charles I and Cromwell the rivals, Anglican and Presbyterian, ever clashed. To a Conservative of the Church of England Cromwell was that "brave bad man," "damned to everlasting fame," who had "wallowed in the blood of many gallant persons." He was "the English monster," the "shame of the British Chronicle," whose "bloody tyranny" quite drowned the names of Nero and Caligula. He had "all the wickedness against which damnation is pronounced, and for which hell-fire is prepared." This was a rather severe arraignment of the "Lord Protector," but the Puritan detractors of Charles I

73

also had the gift of tongues. He was, said Mayhew, "a messenger of Satan to buffet us," a man "black with guilt" and "laden with iniquity." The Puritan preacher ridiculed Charles' rôle as "blessed saint," "royal martyr." He was rather a "burlesque on saintship and martyrdom." With such missiles the Puritan divine fell upon the citadel wherein sat the "dread and fear of Kings."

As the day of wrath and rebellion came upon them, Anglican and Dissenter searched the Scriptures for every sanction of their opposing views. Episcopalian congregations were solemnly warned, "Curse not the King, no, not in thy thought," and were reminded that the King's wrath was "as the roaring of a lion," his favour "as the dew upon the grass." While the divine right of kings and the sanctity of the royal prerogative was being dinned into Episcopalian ears, Dissenters in a neighbouring church were hearing of the parallel between the conduct of Pharaoh and that of George III, and the text was from Proverbs, "As a roaring lion and as a ranging bear so is a wicked ruler over the poor people."

In consequence of opposing interests and political outlook the Anglicans and Dissenters, north of Maryland, at least, took, with some exceptions, opposite sides as the fury of resistance to the King increased. With Judge Jones, a Loyalist historian of New York, the terms Rebels and Loyalists were synonymous with Presbyterian and Episcopalian. Indeed, the Delancey or Tory party there was notoriously Anglican, while the Livingston or Whig faction embraced most Presbyterians, and the election of 1769 was a contest between these leaders, the Tory followed by the mercantile interests and the Anglican Church, while the Whig leader had with him the lawyers and Dissenters. It was said that the Anglican clergy were viewed with "peculiar envy and malignity" by the rebellious element, who even sought an abolition of the Church of England in the colony. In Pennsylvania Galloway found the rebellious spirit "confined to two sets of Dissenters (the Presbyterians and Congregationalists)." Indeed, we need no longer depend upon the general observations of contemporaries, for I have conducted a statistical study, based upon biographical material concerning some four hundred leaders of the Patriot cause, members of Congress, governors of States, emissaries to Europe, generals, all, indeed, of such distinction as to cause the facts of their lives to be preserved. In only two hundred and seventy-four cases could the sectarian affiliation be discovered. Of these one hundred and seventy-nine were either Presbyterian or Congregationalist, thirty-six Dissenters of another stripe, and fifty-six Episcopalians, of whom only fourteen came from north of Maryland. Eighty per cent. of the Patriot leaders were therefore Dissenters. From Sabine's lives of the Loyalists and other sources we learn that over seventy-five per cent. of the Loyalists, whose sectarian bent can be found, were Episcopalian. The total sectarian division among the two revolutionary parties must bear some close relation to these percentages. Indeed, hundreds of contemporaries agree that in the north every Episcopalian was under the suspicion of being a Loyalist, while Dissenters, especially Presbyterians and Congregationalists, were assumed to be Patriots.

One asks, naturally, why in the south, where the Episcopalian Church was established by local law in every colony, as it was not in the north, the members of that Church were not so inclined to embrace the King's cause. The reason is not very obscure. Many planters, strong in their passion for local self-government, fearful of loss of their claims to western lands, or, perhaps, only deeply in debt to English creditors, turned a rebellious face both to the King and the Bishop of London, the spiritual head of the Established Church.

Planters as a rule took their religion lightly, were indifferent to the Sabbath, more given to drink and profanity than were the same class in the north. Their economic interests, therefore, fortified by their political ambitions, overbore any spiritual qualms. In Virginia, even the Anglican clergy, "reputed to roar in a tavern" more effectively than they "babbled in a pulpit," did not so generally hasten to the King's banner as was the case in the northern colonies. Perhaps the loss was not great, for idle curates and fox-hunting parsons were too common, and they were often charged with loose living, and ungodly conversation. The same character was attributed to the Maryland clergy. Dr Chandler wrote ten years before the Revolution, that it would "make the ears of a sober heathen tingle" to hear such stories as he had been told of the Maryland clergy, by many serious people. Only a few good ones "appearing here and there like lights shining in a dark place." Of one hundred Episcopalian ministers in Virginia, eleven were ardent enough in the Patriot cause to become members of Committees of Safety, one became a major-general, and another represented his country in the House of Burgesses. Thirty-four others at least got the repute of being Patriots. Thirteen, of whom

Jonathan Boucher was the most famous, went openly to the royal side, and thirty-nine so carefully concealed their convictions that history may not array them with either side. Methodists, who at that time considered themselves Anglicans seeking to reform the Church from within—were said in Virginia to preach the gospel of passive obedience, preferring to suffer death rather than kill even in war. Men could not "serve Mars and Christ at the same time" was their simple creed. That doctrine did not, of course, make them useful to either side, but was favourable, when held by colonists, to the triumph of the cause of King George.

In South Carolina, as in Virginia, the Anglican Churchmen, though often graduates of Oxford, who had come over the sea as "adventurers" hungry for benefices, joined as a rule the revolutionary cause. Only five out of twenty-three Anglican clergymen became Loyalists. Indeed, in Charleston, most of the leaders of the Revolution were members of old St Philip's, the Anglican Church. Under its lofty arches, looking every Sabbath upon the sepulchral monuments of South Carolina's early royal governors, sat Gadsden, the Laurens—father and son—the Pinckneys, the Rutledges, the Middletons and William Johnson, "rebels all" in the eyes of King George, and in St Michael's Church, another Episcopalian house of God, sat Lynch and William Drayton and another Pinckney, leaders of the struggle for independence which was to rend the British Empire. There were exceptions, however, for an Anglican clergyman in Charleston was dismissed from his congregation for boldly standing in his pulpit and saying that "mechanics and country clowns had no right to dispute about politics, or what kings, lords, and commons had done or might do." Such aristocratic ideas were sternly rebuked by a patriot writer who declared "all such divines should be taught to know that mechanics and country clowns (infamously so-called) are the real and absolute masters of the king, lords and commons and priests, though (with shame be it said) they too often suffer their servants to get upon their backs and ride them most barbarously."

While Anglican Church members in north and south took different lines of conduct in the Revolution, the Presbyterians and Congregationalists of either section were against the King's cause. The Presbyterians were notably active in "sowing sedition." Nicholas Cresswell, an English visitor in Virginia, who had the hard luck to arrive just in time to be interned, and to be made infinite trouble by ardent Patriots, wrote, "The Presbyterian clergy are so particularly active in supporting the measures of Congress from the rostrum, gaining proselytes, persecuting the unbelievers, preaching up the righteousness of their cause and persuading the unthinking populace of the infallibility of success. Some of these religious rascals assert that the Lord will send his angels to assist the injured Americans. They gain great numbers of converts," he sadly concluded. In South Carolina their influence was wholly against the King, and one minister, John Harris, boldly preached revolutionary principles to his congregation, taking his gun into the pulpit, and suspending his powder horn from his neck. He boasted that every man in his flock was a Whig.

Nevertheless, if the North ministry had been better informed as to relations between sea-board and up-country in South Carolina, it might have won the Scotch-Irish Presbyterians of the Piedmont to the King's cause. The British ministry and its military agents, when they invaded the uplands, assumed that the Dissenters there were against government, as in New England, though in truth neglect and oppression of the back country by the ruling Anglican planters of the sea-board had arrayed the west against the east. Only when British invaders destroyed their meeting houses and insulted Presbyterian ministers did the upland forces join the once hated sea-board in resisting the King's army.

In New England, there was no doubt where the Dissenters stood. Ezra Stiles estimates that there were about six hundred Presbyterian and Congregationalist churches in its four provinces, and most of them "spirited their godly hearers to the most violent opposition to government," prostituting their sacred office, in the opinion of Harrison Gray. Earl Percy thought no body of men in Massachusetts so extremely injurious to peace and tranquillity as the clergy, the "Black Regiment," as Otis called them. They sounded the "yells of rebellion in the ears of an ignorant and deluded people," declared Peter Oliver. The able Anglican divine, Samuel Peters, feared his church would fall a victim to the "rage of the Puritan mobility." "Spiritual iniquity rides in high places, with halberts, pistols and swords," he wrote, preachers, on the Sabbath day, leaving their pulpits for gun and drum, "cursing the King and Lord North, General Gage, the bishops and their curates, and the Church of England." Sedition followed from the pulpits, lamented Gage, whence priests "destroyed the harmony of society," instead of preaching the Gospel of Christ.

It was for this that the revolutionary leaders had courted the support of the clergy, bidding them to a banquet in Faneuil Hall, along with the merchants and "Sons of Liberty," and at other times huddling them promiscuously into garrets, with mechanics, lawyers, porters, their fellow patriots. Against just this had Governor Pownal warned Parliament. Arouse the New England clergy, he predicted, and "the spirit of their religion will, like Moses' serpent, devour every other passion and affection." So open was their challenge that the loyal mind was obsessed with their importance as "fire-brands of sedition." The eloquent Gordon was denounced as a "warfaring priest," a "Christian sower of sedition," preaching "carnage and blood." Tory writers described opponents, one as "a deserter from the Church of England," a surly humdrum son of liberty, another's ornaments were "formality and a Presbyterian face."

When a city or territory passed under control of the British army, the Loyalists incited insult and depredation upon Congregational or Presbyterian property. After the British captured Charleston, South Carolina, they used the Congregational Church first as a hospital, then as a store-house and finally as a stable. Near New York the Tories sawed off the steeple of a church, the military men took out the pews and used the sanctuary as a guard-house. In Boston, Old South Church was made a riding school, the pulpit pillar serving as a hitching post. All the tyrants of antiquity were insufficient for Whig descriptions of Gage when Deacon Hubbard's carved pew, with silk upholstery, was taken down and used as a pig-sty. When old North Chapel was scrapped for fuel the Puritan language resources failed altogether. Yet there was quite as much vandalism against Anglican churches in the north when unprotected by British troops. The troops of American cavalry found quarters in an Episcopalian rectory, using the church for a hospital and the pews for firewood. On Long Island Dissenters sent bullets into the Anglican churches, broke windows, stripped off the hangings, stole the leads, and gave them over to unspeakable defilement.

During the Revolution numbers of Episcopalian places of worship were destroyed or left vacant. Their bells had been silent from the first days of Patriot celebrations, while Presbyterian and Congregationalist bells pealed merrily. There was not only passive but very active loyalty in the Church of England fold. A Connecticut Anglican vowed to do his duty, preach and pray for the King, "until the rebels cut out my tongue," and twenty others in that colony urged a peaceful submission to the King. One boasted that of one hundred and thirty families in his two churches, one hundred and ten remained firm friends of government, while "the sparks of civil dissension flew." Little wonder that Whig mobs branded Tories with the sign of the cross, and cried "down with the Church," and that many clergymen were obliged to fly to Howe's army to escape outrage, violence and imprisonment. It was the Episcopalian clergymen, Seabury, Chandler, Cooper and Inglis, who best stated the loyalist political argument, and sought to "stay the progress of sedition." It was necessary when Washington and his army took possession of New York to notify the Episcopalian rector that the General would attend church, and hoped "that violent prayers for the King and royal family" would be omitted.

In the south where many Patriots continued on the Episcopalian path to salvation the state legislative bodies solemnly devoted precious time to cutting out of the service, prayers for royalty and those sentences of the Litany which alluded to His Majesty and the Royal Family, or called on the Lord to "save the King." Even this did not wholly preserve the Episcopalian churches. As the Revolution progressed and the dissenting sects seized the opportunities to sweep away the state support of the favoured church, it was nearly ruined by the loss of tithes, and of its position as a state church. In Virginia, where there had been one hundred and sixty-four Anglican churches and chapels and ninety-one clergymen in 1775, the end of the war found ninety-five parishes extinct or forsaken, and but twenty-eight clergymen remaining. The church was saved at all only because its influence as a buttress of society was appreciated by the planter who still clung to its religious tenets.

The different attitude of Anglican and Dissenter toward the rebellious faction in America was seen in England as well as in the colonies. Two years before the clash at Bunker Hill Franklin wrote from London that he found the Dissenters "all for us," that when the Anglican bishops opposed a Dissenter's petition in behalf of the distressed Americans there had been a spirited reply by one of their number. Lord Harcourt wrote Lord North in October of 1775 that the Presbyterians of the north of Ireland, "who in their hearts are

Americans," gained strength every day. Indeed, until the French entered against England, Protestant Ireland was the most earnestly enlisted on the side of the Americans of any part of the Empire.

On the brink of war, on the other hand, nearly all conservative Anglican forces came to the support of the King and Lord North. Burke thought the Anglican clergy astonishingly warm in their support of the war, animating their flocks to uphold the ministry. Nothing was more natural, for English historians agree that in that generation the Anglican clergy buttressed the favoured classes, preached the insolence of seeking to change the ways of Providence to the advantage of the down-trodden. The order of things which God had plainly sanctioned, like the British *régime* in America, must not be disturbed. Episcopalian rectors in that day, frankly cynical and sceptical, taking theology lightly, accepted the emoluments of not merely one place, but several, resided in none, but leaving residence to half-paid curates, little concerned with religion or the wrath of God. Such men were sure to back the established powers, though there were famous exceptions, like the Bishop of St Asaph. Oxford, never more stagnant or illiberal, dominated by the Church, and seat of inveterate Toryism, as Pitt had found it, gathered the chancellor and masters and scholars in full convocation, to "view with deep concern the pernicious tendency of that profligate licentiousness" which deluded Americans. Betrayed by "seducing arts" they were plunged into civil war with "the state that gave them birth and protection." From the dissenting academies, described by competent contemporaries as "temples of virtue," compared with Oxford and Cambridge, sprang the greatest English defenders of the American cause and philosophy. Richard Price, educated in such an academy, was one of the leading pamphleteers opposed to North's policy. His *Observations on the Nature of Civil Liberty* went through twelve editions in a year and had vast influence on English opinion. Though the Bishop of London attacked Price and his pamphlet in a sermon in the Royal Chapel, the Council of the City of London thanked him and presented him with a gold box of £50 value. America deeply appreciated his services and invited him to become an American citizen, which he gracefully evaded, though he regarded the United States, he averred, as an asylum for the friends of liberty, the hope, the refuge of mankind.

In a political way the sympathy of English Dissenters was little help to America, for the

Dissenters rarely shared in affairs of state, even in local government. Yet their hearts were with the struggling Patriots, as the letter (1784) of a famous English Baptist shows. "I believe all our Baptist ministers in town except two, and most of our brethren in the country, were on the side of the Americans in the late dispute. We wept when the thirsty plains drank the blood of your departed heroes, and the shout of a king was amongst us when your well-fought battles were crowned with victory. And to this hour we believe that the independence of America will for a while secure the liberty of this country; but if that continent had been secured, Britain would not long have been free."

Such is the story of the conflict between Anglican and Dissenter before and during the American Revolution. As groups of men they looked upon life in different ways, though there were many individual exceptions. The Anglican tended to be an aristocrat, guided at least by the rich and great. He was specific, practical, self-interested. The Dissenter, lured by ideals and visions of liberty, pursued theoretical right, and was hospitable to new ideas. The first repelled the zealot and the fanatic, attracted those who were content with the settled order of things, thinking it insolent to seek to change God's ways. The second was full of thoughts of the coming age, seeking the freest forms of political association, aspiring, Utopian, jealous of its liberty. The Anglican, more logical, cared for the state's bodily welfare, admiring strong government which protected property and vested rights, accepting easily the doctrines of submission and obedience to established powers. The Dissenter was turbulent, liked to see the reins of government hang loosely, and feared the dangers of tyranny. Both were useful to the state, each serving with its important function. As an individual the Puritan was severe, self-disciplined, high-spirited, at his best like Milton; the Anglican liberal, generous, form-loving, at his best, cultured, like Sir Thomas Browne. Both Anglican and Dissenter acted at times merely in behalf of his narrow sectarian interests, but each in his best moods gave the noblest of his efforts to the performance of that social service for which he was specially endowed.

Lecture IV

THE INFLUENCE OF ENGLISH AND AMERICAN LAWYERS IN THE AMERICAN REVOLUTION

It would be generally granted, I believe, that it was not the conflict between the "Red-coats" and the "embattled farmers," but that between the political ideals of Lord North and of John Adams which raised the American Revolution to be one of the momentous events in human history. The political theories in the Declaration of Independence had a strange sound in the ears of Lord Mansfield, but they were pleasingly familiar to Thomas Jefferson and his colleagues in the Continental Congress. The greatest significance of the American Revolution, it may be argued, therefore, lay not in the battle of Bunker Hill, the surrender at Saratoga, nor even the fine military stroke which ended the war at Yorktown and severed the British Empire, but in the creation of new forms of government, the invention of that institution, the constitutional convention, wherein the spirit of reforming change which had long ago captured the most aspiring spirits in Western Europe could, on the American frontier of civilized life, embody itself in forms of government, in constitutional principles, consonant with a new and more liberal age.

The men whose activities brought about these changes were in the main American lawyers, while those who held England for a time to the old political paths were the leading representatives of the legal talent of England. While the majority of American lawyers were Whigs, leaders of revolution, those with large practice, and of greatest eminence, became, in the main, Tories, supporters of the British Government. Of eight lawyers having a large practice in the high court of Massachusetts for a decade before the War of Independence, John Adams found only himself and Otis in the Whig or rebel ranks in 1775. Judge Thomas Jones, a great legal figure in New York, became a Loyalist and wrote a notable "Tory" history of the Revolutionary War. Sir John Randolph, Attorney-General in Virginia, adhered to the King's side, and Daniel Dulany, Virginia author of a famous argument against the Stamp Act, became a Loyalist because he could not face the hydra of rebellion. Daniel Leonard, Massachusetts attorney, went with his aristocratic Tory friends, where he would feel most at home with his velvet coat, neckerchiefs and wrist falls of exquisite Irish lace, his satin trousers, and his cocked hat, silver embroidered. The great Joseph Galloway of Philadelphia could not find in his law books any logic to support rebellion, and he too fled to the King's banner.

In 1776 when Generals Gage and Howe held the city with a British army, Boston was the refuge for twenty-four barristers and attorneys, as illustrious as Massachusetts could boast, but Tories all, men to whom came the dream of empire, the vision of an English-speaking people dominating the seas, the immense resources of India, and the fertile valleys of America. World empire, rivalled by none, mingling all that was best of east and west, bringing peace, freedom and industrial growth to all the earth, was the gorgeous prospect which they refused to forsake for a fantastic dream of independence. Some said the colonies would one day have the balance of wealth, numbers and power and the seat of government be removed to America. Then, "some future George might cross the Atlantic" and rule Great Britain by an American Parliament. Either this vision or the nature of their legal training kept them loyal to the Empire.

It is rather remarkable how many American lawyers who remained loyal, or, like John Dickinson and Edward Rutledge, joined the independence struggle after much hesitation and doubt, were trained in the Middle Temple, one of the Inns of Court, in London, where they got a firm foundation in English common and statute law. There were between 1760 and the close of the Revolution, forty-seven from South Carolina, twenty-one from Virginia, sixteen from Maryland, eleven from Pennsylvania, five from New York, and only one or two from the New England states who were thus trained. Graduates of the Middle Temple were slow to turn to natural law, shy of revolution and glittering generalities about immutable laws of Nature. Constitutional resistance within the lines of English law they could support, but once controversy passed beyond, they either went with rebellion, reluctantly like Dickinson, or turned back sadly with Dulany.

While we should not make too much of the tendencies of London-trained American lawyers, it is remarkable how many legal minds, not so educated, led the radical thought in the colonies to ultimate revolt. James Otis, John Adams, Patrick Henry, William Hooper of North Carolina, a pupil of Otis, and many others were home-made lawyers and often very good ones. While most of them had read and discussed in their clubs the great English law writers, there was something in the free frontier life of America which created a natural affinity for the writings of the liberal political philosophers of all ages. Throughout American history the frontier has been hospitable not only to new ideas, but ready to try in a practical way the dreams of the liberal spirits of the past ages. The result is what we would expect on reading in John Adams' naïve diary how his lawyer's club read Locke, Coke, Grotius, Burlamaqui, Vattel and even dabbled in Rousseau. A tabulation of the number of times certain famous political writers were quoted before 1776 by the leaders of the American Revolution, shows Locke leading with twenty-two quotations, Hume, second with twenty, Selden, eleven, Montesquieu, ten, Grotius and Harrington, eight each, Sidney, six, and Vattel and Puffendorf, four each. Indeed, wide acquaintance with such political literature is the one green oasis in the arid desert of American intellectual attainment at that time.

For this reason, added to their vivid political life, the lawyers of Congress could draw up manifestos which led Chatham to assert that he could think of no political expression of any body of men which could rival these papers in solidity of reason, force of sagacity, and wisdom of conclusion. It was, moreover, one of the most serious errors of the British Government to arouse the American lawyers as they did by the Stamp Act. Burke did not fail to point out this folly. The study of law, he said, "renders men acute, inquisitive, dexterous, prompt in attack, ready in defence, full of resources. In other countries, the people, more simple, and of a less mercurial cast, judge of an ill principle in government only by an actual grievance." In America, "they anticipate the evil, and judge of the pressure of the grievance by the badness of the principle. They augur misgovernment at a distance, snuff the approach of tyranny in every tainted breeze."

Of this spirit was James Otis, a genius even in the eyes of his enemies—one whose imagination flamed and whose passions blazed, capable of such a torrent of impetuous eloquence that men left his presence to take up arms. John Adams believed to the day of his death that Otis' oration against the Writs of Assistance breathed into the American nation the breath of life. Another lawyer who could hear from afar the clank of chains was Patrick Henry, the most flaming figure in Virginia history, a hero of the lower classes, whom he was reputed to set against the high-born. He certainly was not liked by the rulers, the clergy nor the upper classes, skilled as he was in coming within a hair's breadth of treason without being actually guilty. "A devil in politics, a son of thunder," but also a "prophet of young freedom," he was one who, when he talked of Caesar having his Brutus and Charles his Cromwell, could be an alarm bell to the disaffected in thirteen provinces, and himself "famous through all the ages." Of much more sober and sound judgment than either was John Adams, who had bent his Puritan mind to the mastery of all the great writers on Government from Harrington to Montesquieu and who longed to be one of that "mighty line of heroes.. who since the beginning of history have done battle for the dignity and happiness of human nature." He would worry a governor into his grave or plan a commonwealth with equal skill and satisfaction. His service in planning America's new political institutions was second to none. It was against such men that were pitted the best legal talent of England.

Though dangerous to press the point too far, it seems true in general that the British statesmen who had least sympathy with America were trained in the law, while those whose sympathy was often shown were not lawyers bred, though they were not ignorant of constitutional questions.

Lord North had studied the German constitution rather deeply, while he was completing his education in Germany; Townshend seems to have read law in Leyden; Grenville, deeply versed in the letter of the law, had a legal training in the Inner Temple, while Lord Mansfield was one of the greatest lawyers of his time, "dignity and reason itself" in the eyes of his admirers, a great master of the British constitution as interpreted by lawyers. Solicitor-General Wedderburn, grilling Franklin before the Privy Council, was showing his mastery of law and invective rather than his good sense and justice. Fox thought his figures and metaphors and legal quibbles cost England a hundred thousand subjects, a hundred million of money, and her American colonies.

William Pitt, on the other hand, a defender of the American cause, never studied at the bar, and though, as John Adams said, he died with the sovereignty of Parliament on his lips, he always refused to come with the law books doubled down in dog-ears to prove the Americans wrong, and even when he did not agree with their ideas about the British Constitution, he refused to fight or tax them to bring them to his way of thinking. Burke was a student of literature and philosophy rather than law, and was more concerned with what "humanity, reason and justice" counselled than what a lawyer told him might be done. Charles James Fox had no legal training. He gave his time to Latin verses, Greek drama, and mathematics when he was not at the gaming table. Law was the least of his affinities. Colonel Barré was a soldier, glaring at North, out of that terribly scarred face, and bidding him keep his hands out of the pockets of the Americans, but offering no legal argument for his not doing so. Lord Rockingham, too, was certainly not a lawyer.

Unfortunately for the unity of the Empire, it was in England an age of strict legalism. As a result, lawyers, dominated by rigid constitutional forms, were most influential in guiding the administration officers in their rule of the colonies. It was they who passed on the form and legality of the colonial charters, and of instructions to governors, and as to the propriety of colonial legislation. The Government preferred to consult them rather than philosophers, and they, ponderous gentlemen of the robe, came to the council chamber with statute books under their arms or in their heads, and tried the fate of nations by forms rather than political expediency. Apparently all but Lord Camden, in 1766, assured the ministry of Parliament's right to tax the colonies. Only Utopians would ask

Parliament to cede its authority to do so. As Lord Littleton put it: "This is no question of expediency, it is a question of sovereignty until the Americans submit" to Parliament. But the majority of American lawyers took a wholly opposite view.

The very terms which English and American lawyers were wont to use in their fierce debates conveyed different ideas to each. If representation was their theme, they had a different theory and practice. If the extent and character of local self-government was the subject of debate, or the distribution of authority between Parliament and some colonial legislature, they used the same words but the ideas evoked were wholly different. If discussion turned upon the extent to which Parliament could constitutionally interfere with the rights of the individual, whether that body was all-powerful or bound by certain unchanging laws of right and wrong, each debater came to doubt the honesty of the other, because each dressed in like phrases different thoughts, the natural results of a varied past.

There was great contrast in the matter of representation. The English member of Parliament was chosen for his seat by any constituency in the realm, while America favoured a representative resident in the district he represented. William

Pitt represented one rotten borough after another, and, never being forced to truckle to win the favour of some local constituency where he happened to dwell, could keep the "strength of his thunder, the splendour of his lightning" for the good of the Empire. In the American system the representative was too apt to look unduly at local affairs, ever fearful of his "fences." Another English characteristic was the franchise, greatly limited by custom and precedent. Even the forty shilling free-holders of the county were often moved like puppets at the polls by great landholders. Though America had not yet given the vote to "every biped of the forest" there were few limitations which enterprise could not remove. In England the franchise was an historical accident, in America a growth in accord with a system. In England voters seemed born as to the purple, in America, the prize was within the reach of all, though by no means everybody enjoyed it; only about one in fifty in New England.

It was in the matter of proportional representation that the parts of the Empire differed most. America believed in it, and any peopled district to which it was denied showed great resentment, as in western Pennsylvania and North Carolina, but England had never made any attempt to apportion representation to the number of inhabitants in any district. Ten southern counties with three million people had nearly as many members as thirty northern counties with eight million. The King, a few lords and landed gentry —one hundred and fifty persons in all—named three hundred and seven members of the Commons, and they haggled and chaffered like market women over their wares. The rottenness of the borough representation is too odorous and too complicated to display here. The mere name "Old Sarum" will recall enough unsavoury associations to serve our purpose. The thing to notice is that the ignorant masses of great manufacturing centres like unrepresented Manchester were indifferent. If a faint cry for reform was heard it was answered that Parliament represented not men but estates—lawyers, doctors, commercial classes, landed gentry. As there were already representatives of commerce, why should Manchester bother to elect more? The American reply was that if Manchester was not represented "it ought to be," and it was in that expression that the most dangerous difference in American and English ideals was to be found.

The American was asking more "rights" than were enjoyed in England. He had no conception of the limits of the "liberty" enjoyed by the masses of Englishmen whose rights he coveted and claimed for his own. He was not contented with the kind of representation which satisfied most English people. Few Americans could conceive of a Parliament so dedicated to the uses of a privileged class as was the actual one at Westminster. There was no proper publicity for the conduct of Parliament. There was no glass hive, as to-day, where the political bees work under jealous eyes. It was rather a breach of privilege to give division lists to the public, or to report debates. No appeal to the "common herd" was necessary, and representatives of the privileged classes worked in secret for their interests, or scrambled for sordid ends, safe from the vengeance of public opinion.

Few Americans appreciated the extent to which British traditions were feudal and aristocratic. All British institutions were in the control of a landed aristocracy, protected by laws as feudal in character as existed anywhere in Europe. The laws and governmental policies were dominated by these landowners and the great capitalists, and buttressed by lawyers whose interests were closely bound to these favoured classes. To all this *régime*, Parliament, chosen under the "virtual representation" idea, was devoted. As far as the British Constitution was concerned, the Americans did have "virtual representation," but they found it, as Pitt said: "the most contemptible idea that ever entered into the head of man." The great Mansfield might say that to change the system of representation would be to change the British Constitution, and ask with a sneer if they would "remodel that, too," but the Adamses would proceed even to that sacrilege. Moreover, they would suffer no change, which meant sending representatives three thousand miles over sea. God had joined taxation and representation, and no British Parliament could separate them, but, in England, that phrase meant only that neither King George nor his ministers could lay a tax without getting the consent of Parliament, while in America only the assembly, elected by those to be taxed, could exercise such power. Thus was the gulf fixed between two opposing principles.

British conservative and American radical had another bone of contention, a difference of opinion as to the relative powers of Parliament and a colonial legislature. Mansfield held that colonial legislatures existed at the will of Parliament, to be scolded, prorogued, dissolved, at the whim of a British ministry. South Carolina's

Assembly expressed the American ideas on that matter, when it claimed the same rights, powers, and privileges, in regard to passing laws to tax the people of the colony, as the House of Commons have in passing laws taxing the people of England. In Mansfield's mind, political power, sovereignty, resided at the centre, in Parliament, a senate "regulating the eastern and western worlds at once." "The Romans were but triflers to us," said Walpole with a flourish. There was but one Parliament over all those British dominions on which the sun never set. Nonsense, replied Samuel Adams, Massachusetts is a perfect state, no other wise dependent upon Great Britain than by having the same King. There are fourteen parliaments in the Empire, one at Westminster, thirteen more in the several capitals of the thirteen colonies.

There the rival lawyers stood and would not budge, each sincere in his conception of the Empire, amazed at the impudence of the other. It mattered not whether deep researches into legal history would prove one or the other to be right; the essential thing for the fate of the Empire was that two opposing theories of it had grown up and could not be reconciled. Each, Briton and American, would cling to his faith until the Empire was rent in twain. Logic and legal precedent would beat in vain against American convictions, formed under frontier experiences, in a new land, far from Westminster where law and precedent were sacred. Judge Mansfield might not be able to draw a line for bounding the authority of the British legislature, but with the assistance of General George Washington and England's European enemies, the American lawyers could draw such a line.

All that could have saved the situation, perhaps, was Burke's proposal. He did not wish "to impair the smallest particle" of Parliament's supreme authority, but one must use sense. Even despotism Burke declared must "truck and huckster." The Sultan, even, only got such obedience as he could, governing with a loose rein that he might govern at all. Burke would have America obey the British Constitution in its own way. The spirit of the Constitution, he believed, infused "through the mighty mass," uniting, invigorating, vivifying every part of the Empire, down to the smallest member.

But lawyers only sneered at such sentimentality. What, they asked, would British ancestors say from the depths of the tomb if "rebels" robbed Parliament of supremacy? Was not taxation the best attribute of sovereignty? Pitt was quite wrong in thinking he could raise up "an host innumerable" among the dead members of Parliament to maintain with their blood the American doctrines. The dead would have listened even more amazed than living members as they heard the words that issued out of the mouths of colonial orators—"silly and mad ideas," which led people to rebellion and overturned empires.

We see, therefore, that at the close of her glorious victories in the Seven Years' War, England met the problem of imperial organization, never faced before, how to distribute authority between the centre and the parts. In practice they actually had a federal system, wherein powers of government were fairly well separated, where Parliament and colonial legislatures exercised their proper quotas of authority, and kept within their own spheres, except for the disputed right of Parliament to exact money for imperial use. All that was needed was a working, legal basis, an acknowledgment of the practice in the theory of the constitution. What was needed was the spirit of compromise. Though England was the greatest of colonizing nations, she had not yet solved the problem of breeding democracies that would be loyal to her. The experience of mankind did not yet offer sufficient light. England and the world had yet much to learn, which only experience could impart. It was true that Americans took their rights "from the same origin and fountain, from whence they flow to all Englishmen," from Magna Charta and natural rights, but new conditions on the American frontier, new needs of the governed, had developed a new political mind, which thought in channels unfamiliar to the English legal expert.

When smart young lawyers in the colonies clambered up to the judgment seat to tell British statesmen how to rule the greatest of empires, or set out to argue down offensive acts of Parliament, they sometimes found that Magna Charta, the Bill of Rights, and even colonial charters failed them. Their refuge then was to natural rights, imitating Pym and Hampden by claiming to be already vested with rights which in truth they were just then seeking to acquire. In doing this, they brought out the third difference between the prevailing colonial theory of the British Constitution and that which was coming to be most widely held in England. It had to do with the extent of Parliament's power over the individual citizen. Samuel Adams, upon whom the shadow of dubiety never rested, declared: "In all free states the Constitution is fixed." He thought it the glory of the British "that their constitution hath its foundations in the immutable laws of Nature." Since both King and Parliament got their power from that source no laws could be made or executed "that are repugnant to any essential law in Nature."

Such an idea was full of promise for a people faced with the threat of absolute rule by a Parliament far away beyond the seas, a legislative body in which they had no voice. But the unsympathetic English lords described this theory as "destructive of all government." Yet, they said, "that wild idea has spread itself over all our North American colonies, that the obedience of the subject is not due to the laws and legislature of the realm further than he, in his private judgment, shall think it conformable to the ideas he has formed of a free constitution." Their best legal minds rejected such dangerous doctrines. The British Constitution, they said, is the Magna Charta, the Bill of Rights, the Common Law as the courts have made it, but, in addition, it is the changing law of Parliament— one thing to-day, another thing to-morrow. "What Parliament doth no power on earth can undo" wrote Blackstone.

Only lately had England acquired the political

habit of accepting the supremacy of Parliament, and that, because it was a way to escape arbitrary rule by the King. Indeed, Englishmen had perhaps not fully grasped the fact that Parliament had power to alter the very Constitution by its changing laws. Some saw it and deplored such power. John Cartwright, a reformer of this period, stoutly asserted that the British Constitution "should be written and taught to children with the Lord's Prayer and the Ten Commandments." Lord Camden, however, believed with Samuel Adams that the Constitution as it then stood was "founded on the eternal and immutable laws of Nature," that American taxation was not legal, and that a mere act of Parliament could not change the Constitution to make it so.

These ideas, opposed to the prevailing legal opinion of England, illustrate the fact that the American Revolution was politically a civil war within the British Empire—not merely between England and America, but between factions in both countries. There were American Tories who upheld Mansfield's conception of the British Constitution, and, in England, Lord North's supporters clashed not alone with Cartwright and Camden, but with Pitt and Burke and Fox, who would not revise the Constitution, but would let the colonists think as they wished, and have their own way, merely because that was expedient and better political sense. Such talk was "sheer madness" to Lord North and George III. The American talk of "unconstitutionality" seemed, to British law-makers and British officialdom, a denial of their legislative and executive authority, and seemed so preposterous that it only stirred their anger and fixed their determination. No British ruler in his heart wished to oppress the Americans, nor believed he was actually doing so. Vowing this, and assuming an air of superiority, together with a certain superciliousness and condescension, did not mend matters.

Had Burke's and Pitt's policy prevailed the unity of the Empire might have been preserved, but, certainly, not the existing character of the British Constitution. Americans loved it, boasted of English traditions of freedom, English liberty, second to none in the world. John Adams held it superior to all other forms of government. "Liberty is its end, its use, its designation, drift and scope" ran his eulogy. Samuel Adams thought no other form of government so fitted to preserve the blessing of liberty, to secure to men the good of civil society. James Otis believed it the most perfect form of which depraved human nature was capable. Yet what the Adamses and Otis loved was not the British Constitution but their idea of it. American and English political thought had come to the parting of the ways. A segment of Anglo-Saxon political life was breaking off, evolving a new organism with new methods of attaining free government. Appreciating this, there is no more reason to regret the separation of the American part of the British Empire, than there is to regret that a new child has been born into the world, different from its parents, destined, perhaps, to give a new trend to human thought or to the habits of mankind. Though America and England had political principles springing from a common source, though much alike in their ideals of liberty, and used to common measures of social justice, yet historical experiences, different environments, had brought forth contrasting methods of securing and enjoying political liberty. Compromise would have been difficult, probably impossible, and it was best, surely, for the highest good of free institutions that each idea should freely work out its logical political forms.

The ultimate differences are easily seen. In England all political power is in the hands of government, though the ministry which exercises that power is easily overthrown by a dissatisfied people. In America, with written constitutions and judicial review of legislative acts, all government is of limited authority, though its agents are not so quickly or easily displaced when disobedient to the will of the people. Each system has its merits, each its disadvantages. Lord Bryce put it finely when, in the inaugural lecture for the Watson Chair, comparing the British scheme of government with the American scheme, he said, "the British excelled in a concentration of power which permitted swift and decided action, while the merit of the American consisted in the safeguards it provided against ill-considered action or the usurpation by either department of the proper function of the other." One was built for speed and the other for safety. By one, decisions can be reached with the minimum of delay; the other averts the risk of decisions not representing the true will of the majority of the people.

It was a common theme of America's defenders in England that her cause was England's cause, that Washington and Greene were fighting for England as for themselves. "Happy Britons," said one, "if they shall owe the revival of their liberty to the success of their American brethren." Englishmen, creators of political liberty on the scale of the great nation-state, as Greece on the smaller scale of the city-state, seemed for the moment to lag behind their own colonists in the race toward human freedom.

The British Empire was broken asunder partly by the insistent demand of Englishmen in America for the full enjoyment of those liberties fostered in England beyond any other country, and partly because the colonial frontier community, hospitable to new ideas, trying new experiments in government, had invented new ideas as to the nature of the British Constitution. But those new ideas were not workable without many modifications. The American leaders made some serious mistakes in their new state constitutions, created during the American Revolution, but their first effort, in the Articles of Confederation, to put into effect what they thought the imperial organization should be, was a monumental failure. Only after years of dangerous experiment did they find in 1787 at Philadelphia the solution now embodied in the Federal Constitution.

The making of state constitutions was the first venture in creating new political worlds. It was John Adams, the Boston lawyer, who brought the most skilled hand to the "manufacture of governments." He was widely read in political philosophy; Locke, Sidney, Vattel, were his favourite reading. Yet he was very cautious, never letting go the thread of experience as his guide in the labyrinth of political change. In the substitution of democratic forms for the old monarchical ones, he and his fellow "constitution-mongers" used the social compact idea, that the people's will might be discovered. The constitution thus created stated the objects and the limitations of government, and did not leave them to caprice or tradition or the momentary will of legislators. There was no reckless abandonment of long-tried political methods, in use either in England or the colonies. The colonial representative system was good and was used, but they deprived the executive of undue power. Fearful of titled aristocracy they stopped the growth of a privileged class, striking at both entail and primogeniture. No man, they declared, should ever get the idea that he was born ruler and governor of others, and the principle that all men were created free and equal, as far as their subjection to law was concerned, was embodied in all the new constitutions. Another of their great concerns was to protect the "natural rights" of the individual against encroachment by the government. A "bill of rights" listed those upon which men could agree.

With these principles as their guide, eleven colonies erected new constitutional fabrics on the foundations of their old colonial charters. Connecticut and Rhode Island went on with the old instruments of government. Though the new constitutions seriously hampered the executive, left much to be desired in the franchise, and did not always separate Church and State, the budding American statesmen were fairly successful in this small-scale state-building.

It was when Congress set out to draw Articles of Confederation that magnificent failure characterized their efforts. They tried to put into actual governmental forms their idea of the proper relation of the centre to the parts in an imperial organization. They only succeeded in creating the best imitation of a government ever struck off by the hand and brain of man. The central government, the Congress of the Confederation, was not given the power to tax, nor the power to regulate commerce, just the powers which had been denied the British Government by the revolutionary colonists. Moreover, the new Congress was not given the power to act directly upon the individual citizen, but only to ask the states of the Confederation to compel their citizens to obey the laws of Congress. Like the famous pirate who put to sea with the ten commandments, but left out one—"Thou shalt not steal"—the absolutely necessary powers without which no government could long exist, were omitted.

A few years of ever-growing anarchy forced all reasonable men to acknowledge the failure of such a system, and the need of a new convention to devise some sort of federal system which would work, and would be accepted. It was just this end that the Federal Convention of 1787 accomplished, but only by giving to the central government the power to tax, to regulate commerce, and to act directly through the courts upon the individual citizen. In this way were the American legal minds obliged to admit in part the pre-revolutionary constitutional contentions of their rivals in England.

Thus was completed the political cycle, which began in 1763 when Great Britain met, and failed to solve in time, her intricate problem of imperial organization, a cycle which ended when America, after one failure, succeeded in solving at Philadelphia, 1787, the like problem of binding together thirteen states, retaining a large measure of self-government but yielding certain essential powers to a central government. Great Britain, too, was to solve that great problem in her own way by a series of changes in her imperial system which ended in the Imperial Conference of 1926, and the ultimate embodiment in written form of what had before been only a custom accepted by all, but binding none by any written constitution.

His Lordship, the Bishop of London, speaking to the University of Michigan students a few months ago, assured them that, contrary to common American belief, there was not in England the least resentment of America's revolt and separation from the British Empire, that rather they were "jolly glad to get rid of us." Well they might be, for if one contemplates the generations of political agony that would have ensued in the endeavour to create common political institutions out of principles and ideals so diverse—even though they had the same aim and, up to a certain stage, the same origin—it is plain that the English-speaking world has been happier, because each great section of it has been free to work out its own destiny in its own way. It is better, surely, that their bonds should be threads of sentiment rather than political chains which might never cease to gall a little. Their relations will be most desirable when every enlightened Briton thinks of America as a worthy scion of the great English race, and every American can read with approval

those thrilling words of an old Virginian statesman of the last century: "Travel through Russia,
Turkey or Austria," he wrote, "and you will
never see a thing to stir your heart with a wish to
be one of them. Stand in the shadow of the
Pyramids and you will be untouched by one wish
that your blood were Egyptian. Go through
Germany and, while you will find there much to
admire, there will still be something lacking....
Even at Napoleon's tomb, the American is not in
touch with his surroundings. Spain and Italy,
while possessed of a wealth of antique beauty, are
to us only the echoes of a decayed and different
civilization. But, some sunny day in London,
wander through Westminster Abbey and read the
names. Some misty morning in Trafalgar Square,
cast your eyes upward to the form of Nelson, as
he stands there in the fog, with the lions sleeping
at the base of his column. In some leisure hour,
visit the crypt of St Paul's, where the car that bore
Wellington to his rest still stands. Then perhaps
you will appreciate my meaning when I tell you:
There's nothing outside of America which tugs
at an American's heart-strings like the names and
deeds and monuments of Old England."

Lecture V

THE RIVAL SOLDIERS OF ENGLAND
AND AMERICA

Fifty years after the American Revolution, Daniel Webster, an orator never unaware of the feebleness of mere rhetorical flights, asserted that in 1775 "the American colonists raised their flag against a power to which for purposes of foreign conquest and subjugation, Rome in the height of her glory was not to be compared." Britain's "morning drumbeat," he declared, "following the sun and keeping company with the hours, circled the earth daily with one continuous and unbroken strain" of her martial airs. If that was oratorical hyperbole, we may turn to a few historical facts as a measure of the strength of the contestants. Britain had five times the resources for cannon fodder possessed by her thirteen colonies. Her fighting marine could muster one hundred ships to America's one. Only a dozen years before Lexington, England's navy had swept her enemies from the seven seas. Her possessions and military posts were soon to dot every quarter of the globe. Her army, in the last war, had carried conquest where it carried colours. In financial resources she surpassed her colonial subjects a thousand-fold, spending in the last war £17,000,000 in a single year. This length of purse was a greater guarantee of victory than the length of sword. A chorus of expert voices warned America that without a single walled town, or disciplined regiment, or a single ship of war, or credit in the money market it was folly to brave the foremost among all the powers on earth. Was England not "the sceptred isle, the seat of Mars"? Not only could America not hope to gain a single battle, wrote the wise ones, but if she were merely abandoned by England, she would be exposed to every maritime power in Europe. Americans must in their weakness have the protection of some powerful naval state for a century to come, said the prophets.

But there were minds both in England and America which considered all the factors and came to different conclusions. Granted that England had the ships, and the men, and the money too, could she use them effectively three thousand miles from her base of supplies? Men have gone round the world in our day in the time it took a transport ship or man-of-war to cross those watery wastes in 1776. The passage was dangerous, too, as the safe passage of only one supply ship during three months of the Siege of Boston testified. Moreover, official corruption often made transport ships little better than floating charnel houses, and, in Keppel's words, not "fit to meet a seaman's eye." In the seven years of the American war seventy-six ships foundered or were wrecked. Some had hulls leaky and worm-eaten, others had bows that might be wave-crushed. They were so small that the fancy of their passengers pictured the waves as "forbidding chains of mountains." To-day in a month's time the *Leviathan* could transport more troops from England to America than could the whole British fleet in a like time during the War of Independence.

When, after braving these conditions of transport across the Atlantic, the British fleet and army sighted the American coast, new troubles arose. Uncertain winds and currents, ill-charted sea-coasts with no lighthouses or other aids to navigation were a terror to every transport fleet, causing delays which upset all estimates of the time required to transfer armies and their equipment. Blockading fleets met the same dangers, yet there was some sense in Lord Barrington's counsel to leave the subjugation of America to the navy, Burke's "winged ministers of vengeance." In spite of John Adams' scorn of even a "wall of brass" along the Atlantic at low watermark, the "happy Arcadia" without any commerce with the outside world would not long have endured a perfect blockade. Life without coffee, wines, punch, sugar and molasses, and unadorned with silk, velvet and lace—though Adams called them trifles in a contest for liberty—would not long have contented America, already developing an avid taste for luxuries. Perhaps the reason Barrington was never heeded was that the trouble started with a British army in Massachusetts which Government, for honour's sake, hoped to extricate with dignity.

When the harassed British commanders had gotten their armies across the waters, past the dangers of the sea-board, and safe on land, military problems of a baffling kind confronted them. Rebellion seemed to be in favour with all the gods. Certainly they placed every obstacle before the armies of King George. Lack of any one place of government or place of military concentration, climate, distances, wide dispersions of the points of military activity gave the British commanders, with only European experience, problems they had not met before. The winter rigours of the north, the torrid summers in the south, malaria over great areas of the sea-board, fought in the main on the side of rebellion. Burgoyne was to find it a land of forests where ground was to be won by inches, where defeat was ruin. Howe after two years of effort had found only large, inaccessible areas defying conquest, and held only stations. Attack had found only empty spaces, American settlements too dispersed to conquer. Only an army of such proportions as Lord North and his ministers never had the imagination to conceive could have swept aside all these difficulties. Even had they grasped the immensity of their task, it is dubious whether they could have gotten the English people behind their plans of conquest. There was no great enthusiasm over fighting their fellow subjects in America.

Current stories of a soldier's life on a transport were enough to deter the stoutest English patriot from enlistment. King and country might need him, but aristocratic officials did nothing to make a soldier's life attractive. Dumb brutes freighted by sea and land are given more thought and shown more mercy to-day than was the lot of the common soldier and sailor in the eighteenth century. Press gangs hustled him on ship-board where the cat, the rattan and the rope's-end cowed him into obedience. There he and his fellows were "pressed and packed like sardines" in bunks between decks, so that in storm, with portholes made tight, they gasped for air as if "buried alive in coffins."

These were the horrors of the night, but the day was often worse. Kicked and caned by the mate or sergeant, branded, pilloried and starved, the soldier arrived at the voyage's end only to be robbed by the purser or paymaster. If he rioted or protested against this beastly treatment it was attributed to the unrest of his wicked heart. If on the voyage he came down with scurvy, from which a little acid fruit might have saved him, he was cared for by an ill-paid ship's surgeon, who had to furnish his own medicines. For food, the soldier on a transport had oatmeal, often sour and weevily, boiled in ship water full of worms which "lay in deep corruption," and was served in "coppers." His daily bread was often full of vermin, his bacon sometimes four or five years old. War profiteers furnished meat that had lain in salt for years. It was under such conditions that English armies must be flung three thousand miles to fight their fellow subjects. So great was the dislike of serving abroad, the horror of the brutal practices in the army, and the aversion to the war on America, that not twenty thousand soldiers of the English breed were available in 1776, and recourse was had to mercenary soldiers from petty German states.

In securing the soldiers of British nativity every device was tried between 1775 and 1781. Having exhausted the expedient of voluntary enlistment with the lure of bounties, North did not scruple to offer pardon to malefactors on condition of joining the army. From that his ministry resorted to impressment and inducing justices of the peace to give over to the recruiting officers idle or indigent men. Meanwhile noblemen, cities, towns rivalled each other in patriotic efforts to raise regiments, so that by all the devices some thirty-one regiments of foot were formed between 1778 and 1781. Recruiting was easier in that period because France had become the enemy in the popular mind.

Nevertheless, it is true that, even before the entry of France into the war, the Howes, with the products of the "man-market" bought from "huckster princes," about which emotional historians and contemporary pamphleteers made so great ado, came to New York in 1776 with the greatest fleet and army that England had ever sent across the seas, greater than Wellington had at Waterloo forty years later when he overcame Napoleon, the master of the art of making war.

And this host was equipped far better than Washington's armies were ever to be during the best days they were fated to see, better armed, better fed, better clothed, superior in all that could be measured by a military expert.

Indeed, it was a finely disciplined army, and its commanders were not cursed, as was Washington, with short-service men who made off home just when they were drilled enough to be useful. They were much more impressive, too, than the ragged "Continentals." With them was all the pride and pomp of war, the ear-piercing fife, the shrill trumpet, the soul-stirring drum. The red coats, the long gaiters, the tallowed queue, the squeezed arms and legs of the British soldier did not improve his shooting, but they gave him a certain pride in being a soldier. From the very start Americans got a wrong idea about British soldiers, for it was generally believed from Maine to Georgia that in the retreat from Lexington "three hundred intrepid rural sons of freedom drove before them more than five times their number of regular, well-appointed troops." Yet the fact was that at Bunker Hill, Brandywine, Monmouth Court, or any field where American and British armies met on anything like equal terms, the "Red coat" proved steady and courageous, capable of the best conduct expected of disciplined troops in that or any age.

During the war the British Government had on its pay-roll anywhere from fifty thousand to two hundred thousand men, but they were never by any means all available for a campaign in America. Though the sea was yet a wall, a moat "against the envy of less happier lands," yet English sovereignty was fraught with danger in every quarter of the globe. Gibraltar, Ireland, the West Indies demanded garrisons, and every captured place in America a force to hold it. When in 1781 Sir Henry Clinton's army was at its high mark he could muster thirty-four thousand men. Though it was a regular army enlisted for long terms, it was dispersed not only in posts in America, but also in the West Indies. Impressive as the figures sometimes were, it was never half the army it might have been, never equal to the task which was set by the actual conditions in America.

Nevertheless, it was not America's greater armies, nor her superior state of military preparedness which worried British students of the martial science. If ever a war in history was entered upon with utter scorn of preparedness it was the war for Independence undertaken by the American colonists. When agricultural America opened the gates of the temple of Janus, it risked closing the ports of every colony to the indispensable manufactured goods of Europe. The English source for all guns, powder and military accoutrements was, of course, cut off, and the British navy was sure to make every effort to stop the importation from other European countries. The utter dearth of every weapon suited to the iron hand of Mars was soon clear to Congress, and the word "gunpowder" sprinkled every page of its early journals, while the gunsmiths from Portsmouth to Savannah blew up their furnaces and hammered away on gun-barrels and flint locks in a vain effort to supply the unwonted demand. Nothing but secret aid from France and the risks undertaken by Dutch merchants made possible the ultimate equipping of the Patriot armies that fought at Trenton and Saratoga.

As far as the potential American armies and the fortifications from which to conduct their operations are concerned, we have, curiously enough, a British official document which affords us the best of information. In 1773 Lord Dartmouth, Secretary for the Colonies, sent to the governor of every colony some forty questions seeking information on almost every phase of military preparedness. By some inscrutable chain of events

ENGLAND AND AMERICA

the replies, collected in two large, vellum-bound
volumes, have come to repose in the William L.
Clements library at the University of Michigan.

From this source we learn that the total population was not far from the usual estimate of three
million, and the number of militia about three
hundred thousand. The period of training of the
militia varied in different colonies from two to
four days out of every year, and such arms as they
had—perhaps a flint lock, twenty bullets and one
pound of powder—were their private property.
Dartmouth's reports showed that in the Quaker
colony no militia had ever been provided by law,
while the "Friends" of New Jersey had refused to
obey the militia law there. In New Hampshire
each town must have two hundred pounds of
bullets, a barrel of powder and three hundred
flints for each sixty militia men. A similar law,
rarely lived up to, was fairly general throughout
the colonies. The report to Dartmouth on American fortification was pleasing reading when the
colonists were in a state of rebellion, but terrifying
if any rival nation were planning an attack. "Not
one fort now," was Virginia's and New Jersey's
reply. New Hampshire had a castle built of stone
but "quite ruinous." Pennsylvania had a half-
finished fort, on an island in the Delaware, to

ward off pirates. Castle William, at Boston, in ill-repair and a few batteries at other Massachusetts ports, was all that colony could boast. Georgia, a danger point, had four forts, and New York made the best showing of all with a fort and batteries at the mouth of the Hudson and forts at Albany and Schenectady. Yet only one of its frontier forts was garrisoned. In all these fortified places there were few cannon, small quantities of powder, nothing that would stand a day before a well-equipped army.

With no better defensive basis than this the Continental Congress began its work. It was hobbled from the first by the ingrained aversion of the colonists to any special taxation to meet an emergency. Moreover, the moral perceptions of the colonists had long been blunted by exclusion from all but the narrower provincial responsibilities of the Empire. It was hard, therefore, even under pressure of war to raise their political *morale* to the pitch of paying for a national purpose. Without money, laws or means of executing them, except through thirteen jealous states, Congress undertook to gather an army made up at first of the militia from various states, and then of volunteers attracted by paper-money bounties. Neither Congress nor the states dared, at first to ask men to enlist for longer than three months. Even the states, whose sovereign power was not questioned, did not venture in 1776 to conscript men, but only to allure with money rewards for enlistment on short terms. These bounties, which started in Massachusetts at ten, ran up to one thousand paper dollars. In Virginia, even twelve thousand dollars could not always buy a soldier. Drafting was reluctantly tried, late in the war, by several states, but with many devices for evasion. Three hundred acres of land and a negro slave were offered as bait in the south. Some got the bounty and refused to serve, while others deserted. To recruit the Continental army Congress gingerly advanced inch by inch from ten dollars in 1776 to two hundred dollars in 1779. The poor results were not due solely to lukewarm love of liberty, nor repugnance to military life, but to a feverish demand, and good pay, for labour and the opportunities to get rich by doing business at war prices. There were fortunes to be gotten by becoming what indignant Patriots called "harpies of trade" or "caterpillars allowed to hang on the branches of commerce."

Americans had in that day the same sublime faith in their ability to raise armies between morn and dewy eve which was to cheer their political demagogues for over one hundred and fifty years thereafter. Confident of mere numbers, they never could be convinced of the truth of the old adage that the wolf is never frightened by the size of a flock of sheep. The members of Congress were no worse than the ordinary unmilitary citizens in their simple belief, but it always paralysed their action when commanders plead for a standing army which might be drilled and disciplined. As a result, the Continental Congress gave Washington impossible tasks to perform with utterly inadequate means. Such armies as he had must be begged partly from Congress, partly from state governments, partly from local committees. In consequence, he received orders from each of these sources often conflicting and sometimes against his better judgment. Always obliged to supplement the inadequate Continental army with the aid of militia, Washington never knew what part of a provincial quota would actually appear, a half, a fifth, a tenth, any fraction might arrive with an equipment as fractional as its numbers. This militia, lent by a state for some nearby campaign undertaken by the Continental army, called out whenever the British threatened any neighbouring point, was supplied by Congress with arms and ammunition, and when the danger ceased, vanished with all accoutrements, which were never seen again. Militia come in, wrote Washington, "you cannot tell how; go out you cannot tell when; act you cannot tell where; consume your provisions; exhaust your stores; and leave you at last in a critical moment." Their pay was paper at the same wage as the Continental soldier, their food requisitioned, and their transportation was by horses and wagons impressed from neighbouring farms.

But irregularity of the service and equipment of the militia were the least of its faults. In the early American armies Montgomery found the men turbulent, mutinous, "the worst stuff imaginable for soldiers," the "privates all generals," so lacking in discipline that neither lashes, fines, pillory, the wooden horse nor drumming out of camp would produce it. There was licentiousness, said Schuyler, not easy to be described, and "scandalous excesses." Men excused because of illness "were foremost in flight and carried off such burdens on their backs as hearty and stout men would labour under." Added to this unfitness, was their utter lack of money and equipment, the military chest exhausted, a mutiny threatened for want of pay, two thousand men without flints, not enough powder to reply to a cannonading. "Powder— powder—ye gods, give us powder!" cried General

Putnam. At times in 1775 Washington was obliged to conceal the state of his army from his own officers, and once in a council of war, when he learned the terrible truth as to the paucity of powder, he sat dumb with amazement for ten minutes.

Washington was ready at times to retire to the back country and "live in a wigwam." He prayed God he might never again witness such dearth of public spirit, want of virtue, stock-jobbing, fertility in all the low arts. Men seemed to wish to be bribed into preserving their liberties. There were too many "summer soldiers and sunshine patriots." In the midst of a campaign the militia, dismayed, intractable, ran off "almost by regiments, by half ones, and by companies at a time"; the roads were "crowded with deserters." There was no limit to the fertility of the soldier's mind in devising pretexts for escaping the service. Washington was tormented by excuses that plowing was to be done, corn to be hoed, hay to be gotten in, that families were neglected, starving, freezing, and must be saved by the bread-winner. Cold weather always brought on "the terrible disorder of home-sickness." "Cicero could not persuade them to tarry" when their time was out. They went, "though their eternal salvation was to be forfeited." Even in the hour of supreme danger they would not wait a few days to save the cause. Not only did men leave ruthlessly at the end of their enlistment terms but sheer desertion was a daily event. Indeed, both the American and British armies suffered to an unusual degree from desertion—so many Irish going over to the British army that a corps of "Roman Catholic Volunteers" was formed of them, and there was a like flow from the British to the American army until a regiment of them was also proposed.

There was desertion even in the midst of battle. The Petition of some militia men from Amherst County, Virginia, who had fled disgracefully during the battle of Camden reveals facts as to their experience which were doubtless common to such companies everywhere in America. They expressed their shame and sorrow for their conduct and without trying to justify themselves they hoped at least to soften the judgment of the House of Delegates. They had never been sent so far from home, and on arrival in North Carolina (Hillsborough), they rested a short time, and then were marched almost day and night, on half allowance of flour, for eight or ten days. They had previously had no military discipline and no time to learn. Exhausted and fatigued by the heat, dispirited for want of rest and diet, panic-struck by the noise and terror of battle, entirely new to most of them, they had fled despite every effort of the regular officers. Their inexperienced militia officers drew them up in too close formation and did not permit them to fire until the enemy fired—a terrible ordeal even to the veteran and well-drilled soldier. Such were their excuses, and even the hardiest chimney-corner warrior must admit that under such conditions of preparedness their flight was natural enough. General Morgan knew better how to use his militia. Blamed by Greene for fighting in the open country and not protecting his flank by a marsh, he replied, "I would not have had a swamp in the view of my militia on any consideration; they would have made for it, and nothing could have detained them from it."

Worse military traditions or greater prejudices against the discipline of war would have been hard to find. Washington pleaded in vain for a standing army, for long term enlistments. All tradition was against it. Because of a "levelling" spirit his officers could not command, but must win with argument or fire, with example or whisky. Some were said to be insubordinate even under guard. Greene told Lafayette that "mild laws, a people not used to prompt obedience, a want of provisions" and all means of getting them, rendered an officer's orders ineffectual. This, he said, "obliges us to temporize, and when we cannot accomplish our object in one way to attempt it in another."

There was little glamour in the American army to lead men on to glory. "Shoeless tatterdemalions," with no uniform but a hunting shirt, butternut stained, could not experience pride in showy dress, the thrill of being part of a gorgeous pageant. The buff and blue uniform in which popular fancy arrays its revolutionary ancestors was a rare adornment of the real hero of '76. Washington reported his own camp servant "indecently and shamefully naked." Greene in 1780 wrote Lafayette of his ragged, half-starved troops destitute of everything necessary for either comfort or convenience, and as a result so addicted to plundering that the utmost efforts of their officers could not restrain them. During the retreat through the Jerseys, Washington wrote that he might "almost as well attempt to remove Mount Atlas as to try to stop the plundering." Four years later he declared his troops were "half-starved, imperfectly clothed, riotous, robbing the country people of their subsistence from sheer necessity." "We are constantly on the point of

starving for want of provisions." Mutiny and
sedition were everywhere, dissatisfaction never
so general and alarming, the country in general in
a state of insensibility and indifference. There is
no escaping the truth that heroic soldiers suffered
at Valley Forge because too many people at home
were neither heroic nor unselfish enough to support the war.

That there was a small nucleus of truly heroic
soldiers not even the most cynical historian could
deny. Such men were, like Washington, un-
shaken by neglect, suffering or any ill that war
might heap on life. The virtues of the best of
American soldiers were like those of Cromwell
who "made not money but what they took for
public felicity to be their end." They fought, said
a British admirer, for their altars and their fires
and not for three shillings and sixpence per week,
as did the mercenaries. Moreover, the most inspired patriots were in a state of mind to believe
that the kingdom of Heaven could be carried by
storm, and were sure they were fighting the battles
of the Lord. Men of this type came from every
walk of life and from the peoples of many lands.
All the efforts of race-warped historians have
failed to prove any monopoly of military glory
won by a particular nationality in the American

army. In the Patriot ranks could be found most western European races—Dutch, English, French, German, Irish, Jews and Scotch. The records did not distinguish Scotch-Irish of the Presbyterian sect from the Catholic Irish. The army's composition was about as diversified as that of the British, and the elements, except for the French on the American side in the later years, curiously like-proportioned.

American militia did well in border warfare, fought valiantly to defend farm and village. They could raid and skirmish, but for the "plumed troop and the big wars" they were little fit. Fighting red-skins in the forest was their main experience, and some frontier riflemen were deadly shots at three hundred yards. Individual patriot soldiers were often brave, accustomed to long journeys, used to shooting game in a semi-wild country. After Thomas Paine's *Common Sense* had dealt its seditious blow to royalty most of these forest bred soldiers were men like Cromwell, who would "meet a king in battle and fire a pistol at him as at any man."

The contempt of the British officer for the American soldier was due to a wholly wrong standard of measurement. Even the immortal Wolfe wrote them down as the "dirtiest, most contemptible cowardly dogs that you can conceive. There is no depending on them in action. They fall down dead in their own dirt and desert by battalions, officers and all." Nicholas Cresswell, an English observer of the early American army, found it "ragged, dirty, sickly and ill-disciplined," and could not believe that his countrymen could be "beaten by these ragamuffins." It was commonly believed in London that "one British soldier would beat six Yankees," that they would fly away and caw like crows at the smell of gunpowder. Wolfe, as others, forgot their lack of drill and discipline, without which the bravest would display the white feather before the murderous fire of battle, and they considered too little, also, the backwoods method of fighting behind a tree or in a ditch which was destined in the future to take the place of the old serried ranks marching up and pouring shot into each other.

After Bunker Hill, Gage, who had been sure they would be "very weak," lions only if the British were lambs, admitted that "the rebels were not the despicable rabble" he had supposed, and even Lord Sandwich talked less about "dastardly, hypocritical cowards," "skulking assassins" not daring to look a soldier in the face. Yet even on the famous hill not all Yankees were heroes. An

eyewitness tells of parties of men ever hurrying to
the rear pretending to carry the wounded, twenty
hovering about one disabled man, unable even to
touch him. But most of them had never been
under fire before, and they had had only a few
weeks of drill and discipline. There was every
latent possibility in the Americans to make the best
of soldiers, but they were hard to develop under
the actual conditions. Short terms, not long
enough for proper training, defeated all efforts to
that end. Even the fires of patriotism died out of
men, "fed with promises," clothed "with filthy
rags," sleeping on rain-soaked ground. Even
better trained soldiers might have failed, and it
was little wonder that raw militia fled before
regulars, as they always have since time began. If
we remember the poor pay, often six months in
arrears, the incredible hardships, cold, hunger,
the almost hopeless outlook, the first absence from
home, stark defeat which sickened the hearts even
of heroes, we may better understand the deserter,
the malingerer, the coward, even the traitor.
Added to all other ills, the soldiers, we must remember, listened to ghastly tales of a hospital
service, badly organized, ill-supplied, dishonestly
administered. They saw camps where thousands
of sick went uncared for in scenes of suffering and

death. And one must bear in mind those who did endure to the end, who suffered the flight through the Jerseys, the winter at Valley Forge, who in spite of the almost continual defeat kept the fires of hope burning. Well might Washington say in his farewell orders, 1783, "the unparalleled perseverance of the armies of the United States through almost every possible suffering and discouragement for the space of eight long years, was little short of a standing miracle."

Such was the nature of the common soldier in the opposing armies. The character of the officers on either side is quite as significant for explaining their conduct on the field of battle. North was not making a mere sorry jest when he declared he did not know whether the British generals would frighten the enemy, but he was sure they frightened him when he thought of them. Though England had the memory of a Marlborough and though a Wellington was to rise in time to meet Napoleon, there was no military genius living to undertake this "ugly job." Carleton saved Canada, Hastings India, but in the thirteen colonies no general arose equal to his task. Sir William Howe, though he had condemned North's American policy, was urged because of his brilliant record in the Seven Years' War to replace Gage at Boston. He accepted, went to Boston in time to play an heroic part in the battle of Bunker Hill, and he and his brother Richard, Lord Howe, came to New York with an imposing fleet and army. There they conducted a campaign which had brilliant features, but which ended in failure, because of conduct which has been a historical riddle from that day to this. The Howes were accused of being mere tools of Burke and Pitt and Camden, opponents of the war. Perhaps they had been ordered to have the olive branch in one hand and the sword in the other. Critics who liked scandal talked of a "wanton with a velvet brow," who cost Sir William the honour and the glory he might have won. The Lord, it was said, sent a Delilah to shear away the strength of the British Samson. Yet in tactics and strategy he showed the hand of a master, attention to every detail, easily carrying to success all that he seriously attempted. If women, wine and the card table unnerved this modern Antony, they did not prevent his being a master of his art, whenever he chose to attend to it. He knew his military science as far as books gave it, but he wanted energy or any ray of genius. He would leave no military device untried in pursuit of Washington, but seemed to take pains never actually to seize his prey, calculating with "the greatest accuracy the exact time necessary for his enemy to make his escape." Even Washington, who reaped the benefit, criticized him for his inactivity, when with immensely superior forces he showed no vigilance, no enterprise, scattered his army, sat around waiting for rivers to freeze, awaiting a blow. He was always, like Austria, "just behind with an army or an idea."

A year later he failed to join Burgoyne, though the fate of an army depended, and went with the aid of his brother's fleet to Philadelphia by way of the Chesapeake, and spent a winter of pleasure there until he was recalled in the following spring.

To Howe succeeded Sir Henry Clinton, a hero at Bunker Hill, a distinguished officer in the Battle of Long Island, but wholly inactive, except for a policy of petty raids, when he became the head of the army. The Earl of Cornwallis, second in command, could not goad him to undertake large plans. "No use sticking to our salt pork at New York," Cornwallis sneered, "sending now and then a detachment to steal tobacco." A Southern campaign was finally undertaken, with Cornwallis fairly successful until he was at last compelled to surrender an army at Yorktown because Clinton did not show the vigour nor good sense to come to the rescue with both fleet and army. In the

William L. Clements library there are minutes of a council of war held by Clinton for six weeks preceding the capitulation at Yorktown, which show Clinton holding out against every one of his officers in the policy which led straight to the surrender and the loss of America. Though it was Cornwallis who lost the army, his countrymen did not hold it against him, and later in India, he won, if not glory, at least the reputation of a statesman, an able general and a gentleman.

In the British army were many officers who were members of great families, and there was a wide gulf between them and their men. They were students of military science, and sometimes, as in the case of Cornwallis, very excellent leaders of men. In general their effectiveness was lowered by the vicious custom of buying and selling commissions with no regard to the aspirant's martial fitness. Though Wolfe called British military education the worst in Europe, it is an open question whether English officers or those of their German allies were superior in military knowledge and training. Both before and during the war, in the occupied towns, these officers aroused the jealousy of the colonial patriots and nettled their sensitive pride by an attitude of tranquil superiority. In a puritan community they were likely to shock the good provincials by their cosmopolitan pleasures, getting drunk of an evening "for the honour of St George," and at the play-house making the audience chorus "God save the King," "Britains strike home" or "Rule Britannia." Then with a band they would march through the streets, having drunk as hard as they could "to keep out the cold," and sing under the window of some lady whom they wished to compliment. Yet liberal-minded persons wrote of them as men of decent morals, and of a judicious and moderate way of thinking.

The British officer in Boston resented being called an instrument of tyranny, knowing as he did that many of the best citizens welcomed his presence. He did not object to fighting the Whig armies after sitting in loyal Boston homes and hearing with horror the tales of persecution by Whig mobs. Peace-loving, loyal Americans, whose crime was signing an address to Governor Hutchinson, told sympathetic British officers of boycotts, threats, tar and feathers, mutilated cattle, and battered homes. The officers saw only one side, and recoiled in horror from such a barbarous people. As the "Redcoat" looked about him on a prosperous land enriched by the labour and savings of Englishmen freer than those in the

British Isles, he could only sneer at talk about tyranny "worse than that of the dark ages in its savage barbarity." The uproar about slavery and oppression was nonsense in his thinking. Yet this opinion was not unanimous, for General Fitz-patrick, who admired even while he fought, wrote, "There is a greatness and dignity in all the pro-ceedings of this people that makes us contemptible indeed," and he expected the Americans to be-come "the greatest people...in the history of mankind." Of this widely different mind were the British officers who led brave soldiers to ultimate defeat on the American frontier of the British Empire.

It was Washington, the aristocrat, who led America's democratic revolution. There was not yet so much democracy in America but that Con-gress desired a gentleman as a military leader. He must shed lustre on his dignities rather than re-ceive it. The very jealousies among the several sections aided his selection. The colonies outside New England feared that an army largely re-cruited there, if also led by a general from that section, might threaten the very independence of America, and come "to give law to the South and West." To remove all jealousy John Adams moved the choice of the Virginian, George Washington,

147   10-2

who was then elected. Though Charles Lee, the traitor, knew far more of the art of war, of military tactics, and military discipline, and though Benedict Arnold, the other traitor, had more of the dash and initiative of the successful leader, Washington was wisely chosen. His was the strength of character, the unswerving devotion to the cause, the truthfulness which gave him the confidence of diverse peoples who distrusted each other, but trusted him. He had neither brilliance, wit nor imagination, but a sound and vigorous mind, able to make use of those who knew books and the speculations of political thinkers, to see what was best and safest in the thinking of others. He had no genius and little natural aptitude for war, no experience except in frontier warfare, and must learn from day to day, from defeat and success, such military science as he came to have, such qualities as made him before the end of the war one of the foremost among the leaders of men, safe and competent as a commander-in-chief. With such equipment he embarked, as he wrote his brother, "on a wide ocean, boundless in its prospect" with no safe harbour, perhaps, to be found.

Under Washington served as varied a lot of subordinates as ever fought under a brave leader.

Such American officers as had any experience were veterans of the French and Indian wars—a dozen years in retrospect. A few had been trained in the British army—like Montgomery and Charles Lee —while others had a Continental training, as did Conway, De Kalb, Kosciuszko, Von Steuben, and Lafayette. Near the end of the war Rochambeau with the French army came to Washington's aid.

Cromwell expressed a preference for a "plain, russet-coated captain that knows what he fights for and loves what he knows," rather than a mere gentleman, but the Virginian planter had quite a different ideal. Washington, a true aristocrat, believing in gentility and a graded society, said very frankly that he wished none but gentlemen as officers, men with dignity of character, who could use the tone of authority. He desired refinement, sense of honour above self-seeking. He was in despair over the swarms of colonels, officers of the peasant type, demagogues who intrigued for election by their men, willing to chum with a wagon-maker, or be the company barber, if thus they could curry favour. To scorn titles, care nought for military salutes, and to let men draw pay while actually on leave getting in the harvest at home, were ways to win popularity. Some regimental officers, said Washington, driven by scant pay "to low and dirty arts," filched from the public and encouraged their soldiers to do it, even leading plundering expeditions and dividing the stolen goods. The officers, he wrote in 1776, "except in a few instances," were "not worth the bread they eat." In New England the spirit of democracy forced men and officers to the same level, the latter courting election by the lowest arts, and pooling their wages with the men. Even John Adams, "Yankee" democrat as he was, became "wearied to death with the wrangles between military officers high and low. They quarrel like cats and dogs. They worry one another like mastiffs, scrambling for rank and pay like apes for nuts." It took Washington a long while to make such material into brave, steady and efficient officers, but before the end of the war he did it or sent them home in disgrace.

Under Washington were several able subordinates. There was Montgomery, soon to fall before Quebec on the field of glory. There was Nathaniel Greene, fresh from the *Lives of Plutarch* and the *Commentaries of Caesar*, more nearly a military genius than any other American leader. He was not so much a Quaker but that he could extract the best out of every book on war, and the lessons of Fabius best of all. Throughout the war he was Washington's greatest support. There was Benedict Arnold, with dash and verve and an indomitable spirit of adventure, capable of an heroic march that Hannibal might have admired, but wanting in the strength of character to endure steadfast, in spite of persecution and injustice, to the end. And then there was Schuyler, and Charles Lee, Henry Knox and Horatio Gates, and others good or bad, faithful or troublesome, all to be the immediate tools with which Washington must work upon a body of lower officers, rarely trained, often born unfit for such duties. That he succeeded as well as he did is a great tribute to his wisdom, patience, and unswerving devotion to the cause.

As a result of the lack of "preparedness" on either side as understood to-day the scale of battles and campaigns was never great, as such events had often been measured in the past, nor as appraised in the last century. The amazing thing to a novice in revolutionary history is the almost absurdly small forces engaged in famous battles. He finds Washington winning a victory at Trenton with twenty-five hundred men. He reads of Cornwallis at Guilford Court House with only fifteen hundred soldiers, and Greene opposing him with forty-four hundred of whom half were raw militia, wholly dispersed within a few weeks. Morgan won at Cowpens with eight hundred men, and Washington marched from the Hudson to his crowning victory at Yorktown with only two thousand men, reinforced however by four thousand French. One great explanation of this was that only a fraction of the colonial peoples shared Samuel Adams' vision of an independent America, and not all of them cared to fight for it. After the first blaze of wrath over Lexington and Concord, an army of possibly fifty thousand might have been enlisted for the war, but when the patriotic fires of 1776 had ceased to glow, the problem of getting men for the Continental army increased every year, and after the advent of the French army, fighting patriots became even more scarce. Near the end of the war the sources of patriot soldiers nearly dried up. Could the American army on paper have met the actual fighting force under Washington, the scene would have resembled that historic meeting at Thermopylae between the Persian hosts and the little band of Greek heroes under Leonidas. Had half the American population been favourable to the cause of Independence and ready to fight for it, there should have been two hundred and sixty thousand men of military age ready to spring to arms sometime between daylight and dark. From such almost worthless statistics as we have we find less than ninety thousand appear on the paper records in 1776, all on short-time enlistments, yet Washington in that year never could count on much above twenty thousand, sick and unfit included. Even this number—at no time much exceeded—was subject to seasonal variations, to the comings and goings of state militia, to the ebb and flow of minute men, fighting a few days for altars and fires and then returning to their shops and farms. Fortunately for America's success, its army was not merely the armed and disciplined force, obedient throughout the years of war to its patriot leaders, but the ill-trained farmers, citizens, shop-keepers, ready to leave their work and fight when the enemy approached, and forming at all times a potential force far beyond the army in being. It was a nebulous, incalculable, yet occasionally, as at Bennington, a mighty force. The British army was a more palpable force, and it, like the American army, contained its full quota of heroes ready to meet a great occasion in a noble way, but the war itself was of such a nature that neither its scale nor intensity raised it to the rank of one of mankind's greatest struggles. There was nothing so spectacular as Napoleon was to show the world within a generation. Only once or twice in the war is the imagination fired by quick marches, daring attacks, the spirit to die in a hopeless engagement. There was no Marathon, no Bannockburn nor Balaclava, no Old Guard which could die but not surrender. There was the wintry crossing of the Delaware, and swift victory at Trenton; there was the brilliant stroke at Stony Point, the endurance of Washington and his army at Valley Forge, final victory snatched from the jaws of defeat in 1781, but military glory of the kind that thrills the mind of man throughout the coming ages does not shine upon the battlefields of the Revolution.

Lecture VI

THE OPPOSING DIPLOMATS OF
ENGLAND AND AMERICA

When in 1775 England and America faced each
other on the field of Mars, a comparison of their
resources must have convinced even the dullest
observer that the thirteen rebellious colonies could
hope to win independence only through the active
aid of England's enemies in Europe. It was
natural therefore that diplomatic agents from
America and England should at once besiege the
continental courts seeking, or trying to avert, aid
for the American cause. If training for the pro-
fession was to count for anything, never were there
more unequal gladiators in the diplomatic arena.
None of England's ministers in the important
capitals of Europe were amateurs, while every
commissioner sent by America, except Benjamin
Franklin, was the merest tyro, an untrained
"militia" diplomat, who hardly knew the names
of his diplomatic weapons. The British representatives—Lord Stormont in Paris, Baron Grantham in Madrid, Sir Joseph Yorke at The Hague,
Hugh Eliot in Berlin—were experienced if not

always successful diplomats, while Sir James
Harris at St Petersburg was judged in later years
to be the "cleverest diplomat of his time." "It is
useless," said Talleyrand, "to try to surpass him,
one can only follow as near as possible." Compared with this array of trained diplomatic talent,
the American opponents, except the sage old
philosopher who "snatched the lightning from
the skies," were mere clownish imitators. Arthur
Lee, arrogant and suspicious, though loyal himself, employed at least six British spies to act as
his secretaries, and thus betrayed to Lord North
every secret of the commissioners. He so enraged
the French that one of Vergennes' aides swore he
would have shut Lee up in the Bastille but for the
unpleasant results, and Franklin was so pestered
that at last he rebuked Lee for his "jealous,
suspicious, malignant and quarrelsome temper."
You have "schooled and documented" me with
your "magisterial airs" he wrote, "as if I had
been one of your domestics." Ralph Izard, a
gentleman of fortune, violent in temper, rash of
judgment, quarrelled with all his colleagues, and
ended by calling Franklin "a crafty old knave"
and seeking his recall. William Lee, Francis Dana
and William Carmichael were not quite such
troublemakers, but they accomplished nothing.

John Adams was able enough but wanting in all the graces of a diplomat. Taking all into consideration such success as the American mission achieved was due to forces and to international relations which they neither created nor manipulated. The British nation had been too long successful in an envious world, and when its colonies revolted were made to realize the truth of the Indian proverb that all the other tigers are charmed when one tiger loses its tail. Other powers, getting more daring, more pressing as England's troubles grew, demanded settlement of all standing diplomatic questions. As a wise old Quaker wrote, "It seems to be the will of Providence that after we (English) have humbled the pride of the most potent houses in Europe we should be humbled likewise—by our own selves—in our own turn." England, like a strong man fighting with many weaker men, had danger all about, safety only in defence at every point.

Of all European nations France had greatest reason to envy England's favour with the gods. Closing several centuries of almost ceaseless warfare between France and England was the Seven Years' War. At its end, in the Peace of 1763, France lost its commerce and credit in the Indies, it lost Canada, Louisiana, Isle Royale, Acadia and Senegal. It was deeply in debt, its allies

disaffected, its prestige gone in all the courts of
Europe. It was helpless at the time of the parti-
tion of Poland, a mere unheeded onlooker. After
1763, its ambassadors walked at the heels of
British ambassadors at affairs of state in foreign
capitals. Once the centre of all European political
activity, France seemed least considered of all
great powers. "The dogma consecrated by a
thousand years" that France should "give the law
to Europe," that the Bourbon throne was "a
tribunal set up by Providence to settle the rights
of kings," was forgotten, as was France's greatness, antiquity, rôle of leadership, and her tradition of grandeur. All this seemed to have passed
to England. It was sea power, wrote Abbé Raynal,
which had given the universe to Europe, Europe
to England, who thus dominated the states of the
peace world. There was, declared Choiseul, "no
with such a race" which aimed at supremacy
in four quarters of the globe, and the ink was
scarcely dry on the peace parchment when that
French minister set out to reverse the decision of
destiny. He bettered the finance, repaired the
navy, reformed the army, planned in great detail
an invasion of England. He plotted for a league
with Prussia, Russia, Austria and Spain to take
Gibraltar and close to British trade the sea it

guarded. For a decade, French spies roamed over England and America, measuring the British national debt, the size of its army and navy, the significance of its political crises. A French reporter elected to Parliament got the most secret debates. Five hundred guineas a year let the French inside the Colonial office.

In America the spies blew up the coals between Britain and her colonies, dropping insinuations to induce a spirit of discontent. Nothing there escaped their eyes, the plans of forts, the number of the garrison, the children swarming "like broods of ducks in a pond." They rejoiced to find New England restive to shake off the fetters of trade, murmuring against government, and boasting of its power, and yet the spies were chagrined at times to find America "caressing its chains," really loving England. Nevertheless the rebellion, of which Montcalm had dreamed, was coming, they wrote. At taverns they saw the rage against stamp duties augment as the bottle went round. America would soon be on fire, which must not go out for want of fuel. While all this intrigue went on France and England were cordial on the surface, suspicious in secret, reaching the hand of friendship, while scheming with each other's enemies.

In America, all of Choiseul's efforts to blow up

the fire, lying under the ashes, came to nothing. The colonies must be hard pressed, indeed, before they would turn to a Catholic power, perhaps to become the slave of "popish bigotry and superstition." Loyalists especially warned them against the "horrors" of French slavery, the "miseries" of a foreign yoke. Later, when America was driven into the arms of France, loyalist newspapers talked of a French fleet coming with many priests and confessors to convert New England, bringing tons of holy water and casks of consecrated oil. Chests of reliques, beads and crucifixes were on board and quantities of crape shifts, hair-shirts, cowls and scourges. One vessel, it was said, carried only consecrated wafers, crucifixes, rosaries and bales of indulgences. Even heretics were not forgotten, for there were wheels, hooks, shackles and fire-brands. Everything in French customs or character, which was hateful to the Anglo-Saxon, was urged against seeking the aid of "that despotic arbitrary prince," His Most Christian Majesty. Nevertheless, as the war cloud darkened, all these imagined terrors became as nothing compared with the dismay in the heart of every reasoning American as he thought of war with England lacking the aid of France, and any other European power which might be enlisted.

Little by little ancient prejudices melted away, and many patriots began to talk of seeking the friendship of England's enemies. In the fall of 1775, one Bonvouloir appeared in Philadelphia, and induced five members of the Foreign Committee of Congress to come in the dark, by different roads, to a rendezvous where he showed "his hand only a little," disclaiming all right or power but talking darkly of sinews of war from France, hinting, however, that it was slippery business in face of the English. Though evasive, clandestine, underground, he did induce them to take heart and to send Silas Deane, an agent, to buy supplies in France.

Already a group in Congress were talking boldly of seeking European alliances. The Adamses and the Lees having never dwelt in the ivory towers of diplomacy, never wandered in the mazes of eighteenth-century European politics, were all for action. They would use a "blunt simplicity" and teach European governments to know their own interests. "God helps those that help themselves" was their maxim. Ignoring, therefore, the age-long custom of diplomacy that no minister should be pressed upon a foreign power until it was known that he would be welcome, the virgin republic went suitoring after alliances in every country of

Europe—William Lee to Austria, Adams to the Hague, Izard to Florence, Dana to Russia, and Arthur Lee with a sort of roving commission either to Madrid or Berlin.

The sage old diplomat, Franklin, was all against it. He would preserve America's virgin character, and wait with decent dignity for honourable proposals. He was humiliated by the idea of America "running about from court to court begging for money and friendship," sure to be withheld the more eagerly they were solicited. Franklin was quite right, and the only mission that succeeded was his own in France from whose government the American Congress received secret intimations that advances would be received with favour. The Dutch would give no recognition to John Adams until forced at a later date into union with France. Izard not only never got from the Grand Duke of Tuscany the money he sought, but not even an admission that the United States existed. Arthur Lee was stopped on the road to Madrid and turned back with a Spanish flea in his ear. He got to Berlin, but only to have his papers stolen and be treated with insulting cynicism. At a time when Hugh Eliot, the British ambassador, wrote that the Prussian monarchy reminded him "of a vast prison in the centre of which appears the great keeper occupied in the care of his captives," Arthur Lee assiduously courted its monarch's aid for the people who were at war because they demanded more human liberty than was enjoyed by any other inhabitants of the globe. Dana hung around St Petersburg for two years, humiliated and rebuffed and beaten at every point by the astute Sir James Harris, the able British ambassador. Beside the American violation of diplomatic usage, all these countries were enjoying too great benefits as neutrals to risk receiving American envoys and thus almost surely becoming involved in war with England, drunk with its success in the last war, impatient of any resistance. Izard and the others found well-wishers in every capital of Europe, and all the papers pleased with England's troubles, rejoicing that there was still a part of the world where tyranny was not triumphant, but nobody wished to risk anything.

Having failed in all the other missions, these "militia" diplomats, as Adams dubbed them, returned to Paris to give point to the famous epigram that Franklin was sent to the French capital to save his country, but was there surrounded by a guard to see that he did not do too much to save his country. Each of Franklin's colleagues did harm in his own special way. John

Adams, who was the soul of honour, and as eager
for his country's good as any man, was too stern
and uncompromising. He was for "a little apparent stoutness, and a greater air of independence
and boldness." He wanted the French court to
know its place. He was ungracious to the last
degree, and soon acquired a reputation, which he,
a stern Coriolanus, did not especially regret, of
being the most unpopular man in France. Indeed,
he said complacently: "I have long since learned
that a man may give offence to a court to which
he is sent and yet succeed." He doubted whether
a man who was not "depraved in his morals"
could ever be pleasing at a court. This puritanical
philosophy might have broken the alliance with
France but for the immense interests she had at
stake, and but for Franklin's suavity. He, at least,
was not afraid of making thankful acknowledg-
ments to the French King, whom he found taking
pleasure in the thought that there was a generous
benevolence in "assisting an oppressed people,"
and that his action would add to the "glory of his
reign." Such a prince Franklin would treat with
"decency and delicacy," and would express gratitude as not only a duty but a matter of interest.

The train of events by which France was led to
deserve America's gratitude is fairly clear. When

Louis XV died and Choiseul fell from power, he was succeeded by the Count de Vergennes, a more cautious minister, but not less bitter toward England. Of his tendency to hesitate, a rival wrote: "If we asked him for the Grand Vizier's head to-morrow, he would reply that it would be dangerous business, but he would send it to us." Vergennes was eager to restore the prestige of France, and early addressed his royal master in a council of state. "England is the natural enemy of France," he declared, "an enemy at once grasping, ambitious, unjust and perfidious. The cherished purpose of her politics is, if not destruction of France, at least her overthrow, her humiliation, and her ruin." Therefore, France must seize every chance to reduce the power and the greatness of England. "Here is the time," he said after Lexington, "marked out by Providence to deliver the universe from a greedy tyrant which is absorbing all power and all wealth." Yet his fears held him back. He saw the spectre of Chatham whose love of glory might make him arouse England against France, perhaps use the British sea power to seize the French West Indies. There was the man to fear. He might plunge the world in flames. Then there was the spirit of revolt, a moral malady, which might be contagious. Perhaps France had better wait.

Financially she was not fit for war. Even the royal servants were unpaid, and when the King was told that his very valets in the royal livery begged in the streets of Versailles, he replied cynically: "I believe it, they are paid nothing." Finance, the social welfare of France, the good of the royal family argued trumpet-tongued against war, yet the archives were filling with memoirs from nobles, counts, dukes, great ministers of state urging right, honour, French safety, as decorous mantles for attack, open or secret, upon England. It was at this stage that the King and Vergennes were led across the Rubicon of doubt, in part by French public opinion, in part by the tireless zeal and infectious enthusiasm of Caron de Beaumarchais. This son of a humble watch-maker, rising through the use of his wits and a love of intrigue to a place of influence in the French court, first touched the pulse of American life, when, in 1775, he went on a delicate mission to London. Once the spark fired his sensitive spirit, he became almost idolatrous of his "dear Americans," clapped hands for their victories, "trembled" lest the King deny his pleas in their behalf. He showed a certain nobility of character, an heroic fervour for the cause of freedom. In the service of this cause he used all those political arts which he described so well in his *Mariage de Figaro*.

To feign not to know what one knows, and to know all of which one is ignorant, to listen to what one does not comprehend, and not to hear what one listens to, to have power beyond one's strength, to hide often as a grand secret what doesn't exist, to secrete one's self while one sharpens a pen, and to appear very profound when one is really empty and shallow...to melt seals and intercept letters, to attempt to give dignity to the poverty of the means by the importance of the objects.

It was these talents that Beaumarchais brought to America's service.

At a meeting in the home of John Wilkes in London (1775) Beaumarchais was told by Arthur Lee that Congress authorized him to demand a treaty of commerce with France that America might get the indispensable munitions of war. Should France refuse, Lee threatened, America must yield, and then, that the broken parts of the Empire might be cemented by fighting side by side, they would together attack the French and Spanish West Indies. Whether Lee or Beaumarchais invented this preposterous threat we know not, but it was to be immensely effective, for De Kalb, Turgot and St Germain had all warned the King of that danger already. Armed with this story Beaumarchais hastened back across the Channel, sending ahead letter after letter reminding the King that he was responsible to God, to himself, and to a great people, and imploring the "Guardian Angel" of the state for a bare half-hour with Louis XVI. Secret aid was all he urged, and in the name of the glory and prosperity of his reign, Beaumarchais urged the King to realize "the facility of doing, the certainty of success, the immense harvest of glory and tranquillity." "We must aid the Americans" to save our own West Indies, he cried. His plan was ready, he would execute it so that the aid would never become a fire-brand between France and England. He taunted, he threatened, he sophisticated, and at last he won. With a million livres from the royal treasury, Beaumarchais set up the merchant house of Hortalez and Company on one of the boulevards of Paris. With reckless disregard of any prospect of payment, supplies of every kind were hastened to America. The invoices lie in the French foreign archives to-day, and include every conceivable need of an army from brass cannon—some with the King's monogram, we are told—to cartridge boxes, from snare drums to music books, wagon harness to horse combs, 100,000 blankets to garters, opium to alum, and amputating instruments to mortars and pestles. The quantities mentioned in the invoices were far greater than ever arrived in America, but from July of 1776 enough got through to save the American cause.

It was in selecting and despatching these supplies that Silas Deane, first of American emissaries to France, rendered great service. Never was there a more bucolic diplomatic agent. Fearful of English spies, he vowed never to speak with people who spoke English, and Beaumarchais swore he must be the most silent man in France, for he could not speak six consecutive words in French! He imagined himself winning Marie Antoinette to the American cause. Learning that she rode horseback, he urged Congress to send him a fine Narragansett horse or two. He would like also to present her with Rittenhouse's famous collection of birds, or Arnold's collection of insects. Indeed, he thought a few barrels of apples, cranberries and butternuts would help. Such was American diplomatic finesse as shown in the first of her foreign agents.

It was only with the arrival of Franklin, December 1776, that America had a diplomat in France equal in knowledge and resources to Lord Stormont, the British ambassador. Even Franklin was swept along by great historical forces, the interests and animosities of nations, the inevitable consequences of an unalterable past, but at least he won the love of the French people, and created an amiable conception of what passed for a typical American. Thus he wrought until he saw a French people "resting quietly in its ancient chains, intoxicated with the joy of breaking those chains in another hemisphere," its young men ready "to run to the world's end to help a Laplander or a Hottentot." John Adams, the stern Puritan, resented Franklin's complacent acceptance of French standards of morality. He was shocked beyond measure when the old man of seventy years permitted Madame Helvetius, who was older, to kiss him on the forehead, but years later he admitted that Franklin in France was better known, loved and esteemed than Voltaire, his name familiar not only to nobility, clergy and philosophers, but "there was scarcely a peasant, or a citizen, a *valet de chambre*, coachman, or footman, a lady's chambermaid, or a scullion in a kitchen...who did not consider him a friend to humankind."

John Adams himself has best described the emotions of an American diplomat when he first found himself in the French court surrounded by dukes and generals and admirals and fine ladies.

He wrote his wife with some pride how he was ordered to a seat close beside the royal family. The seats on both sides of the hall, arranged like the seats in a theatre, were all full of ladies of the first rank and fashion in the kingdom, and there was no room or place for me, but in the midst of them... room was made and I was situated between two ladies, with rows and ranks of ladies above and below me, and on the right hand and on the left, and ladies only. My dress was a decent French dress, becoming the station I held, but not to be compared to the gold, and diamonds and embroidery about me.... The eyes of all the assembly were turned upon me, and I felt sufficiently humble and mortified, for I was not a proper object for the criticism of such a company. I found myself gazed at, as we in America used to gaze at the Sachems who came to make speeches to us in Congress, but I thought it hard if I could not command as much power of face as one of the chiefs of the Six Nations, and, therefore, determined that I would assume a cheerful countenance, enjoy the scene about me, and observe it as coolly as an astronomer contemplates the stars.

When Louis XVI, in the summer of 1776, began through Beaumarchais to give secret aid to the rebel subjects of a brother king, he salved his royal conscience with the belief that the British had set such a precedent recently in Corsica. The inevitable result was the hastening of the fatal day when he was doomed to the guillotine for the sins and wickedness of his fathers. We know that France, either directly or through foreign merchants whom she encouraged, furnished nine-tenths of all the munitions of war which made Washington able to carry on in 1776 and 1777. French secret aid made possible the American victory at Saratoga by which France herself in the end was to be encouraged to ally herself openly with the American colonies. In doing this France violated every duty of a neutral, as Lord Stormont proved to Vergennes with affidavits, sworn on "the Holy Evangelists of Almighty God," but the French minister trailed him along with promises, evasions, unblushing denials of facts plain as Holy Writ. Urged to use his own vigilance, Stormont sneered that the eyes of Argus would not be enough, and Vergennes replied: "If you had those eyes they would only show you our sincere desire for peace." No diplomat could have succeeded there. The cards were all stacked against him. Comparison of Vergennes' bitter hate of England, expressed in his letters to the King, with his unctuous flattery and assurances to Stormont reveals the amazing duplicity of eighteenth century diplomacy. England preferred a lie to the truth, but she was not deceived. She was most anxious to avoid war with a nation having double her population—a fact rarely given half its weight in considering England's position at that time in international politics.

But at last the day arrived when the French government, overwhelmed with debt, and warned by Turgot to avoid war as the greatest of evils, abandoned the policy of secret aid, so rich in results and costing so little, for a course leading straight to war, ruinous financially, even if won. The root-causes of French support of America we have seen. What was the immediate cause for the French decision after Saratoga? There is a difference of opinion, but my own conviction is that France entered into alliance with the United States in the spring of 1778 because Louis XVI and his ministry were convinced that France was doomed to a war with Great Britain, whether she allied herself with America or not, and that it was wiser to join with America, and thus win her support, rather than to wait for England to make peace with America, and then make war in league with her upon France whose island possessions would lie so completely at their mercy. Whether Vergennes' conviction or his device, the idea of this terrible dilemma seems to have been the reason for the decision of the French cabinet.

Beaumarchais had used the idea of endangered colonies to win the King to the policy of secret aid, and now he was ever at Vergennes' elbow whispering the dangers, furnishing the very phrases, which Vergennes used in letters to the King or to Spain, while he kept a little at a distance and in the background, this "Barber of Seville," too clever not to be used, too low-born to be acknowledged. At last France made the decision—no less than the Decree of Fate to America—to make a commercial treaty and an alliance to hold until American independence should be acknowledged. There was not only the prestige which her alliance gave America, the naval and military aid she furnished, the final bringing of Spain into the struggle, but, of greatest service, that momentary command of the sea off Chesapeake Bay, which made inevitable Cornwallis' surrender at Yorktown and the consequent yielding of American Independence.

The alliance formed, Louis XVI decided to flatter America by sending a minister plenipotentiary, Conrad Alexander Gerard.

"Who would have thought," wrote a bombastic American journalist, "that the American colonies, imperfectly known in Europe a few years ago and claimed by every pettifogging lawyer in the House of Commons, every cobbler in the beer-houses of London, as a part of their property, should to-day receive an ambassador from the most powerful monarchy in Europe."

Certainly the Continental Congress had not expected it, and they were quite flurried over the idea of receiving an ambassador extraordinary. As such bodies always do when they are in trouble, they appointed a committee to consult the books of diplomatic etiquette. From that source the committee devised the following impressive ceremony.

At the time the minister is to receive his audience, two members shall wait upon him in a coach belonging to the States, and the person first named of the two shall return with the minister plenipotentiary or envoy in the coach, giving the minister the right hand and placing himself on the left with the other Member on the first seat. When the minister plenipotentiary or envoy is arrived at the door of the Congress Hall, he shall be introduced to his chair by the two Members, who shall stand at his left hand. When the minister is introduced to his chair by the two Members, he shall sit down. His secretary shall then deliver to the President the letter of his sovereign, which shall be read and translated by the Secretary of Congress. Then the minister shall be announced, at which time the President, the House, and the minister shall rise together. The minister shall then bow to the

President and the House and they to him. The minister and the President shall then bow to each other and be seated, after which the House shall sit down. The minister shall deliver his speech standing. The President and the House shall sit while the minister is delivering his speech. The House shall rise, and the President shall deliver the answer standing. The minister shall stand while the President delivers his answer. Having spoken and being answered, the minister and President shall bow to each other, at which time the House shall bow, and then the minister shall be conducted home.

The loyalists derided all this and one put the whole affair in rhyme:

> From Lewis Monsieur Gerard came
> To Congress in this town, Sir;
> They bowed to him and he to them
> And then they all sat down, Sir.

The French court, meanwhile, was making every effort to bring Spain into the war. Spanish statesmen, however, foresaw exactly what did come to pass in America. If successful in winning independence, the example to Spain's colonies would be very bad, and, moreover, a virile young republic would be sure to be seized with a desire for conquest, would push on resistlessly westward to the Pacific. Baron Grantham, in Madrid, appealed to every fear, and had little trouble at first in defeating the efforts of the American commissioners, Arthur Lee, and, later, Carmichael; but French bids for Spanish aid rose higher and higher until at last even suspicious Spain accepted the bribe, though only so far as to ally herself with France, not with America. An offer to let Spain get what she could west of the Alleghanies, another promising a conquest of Florida, and one even to help regain Minorca, all failed, but when France agreed to fight by Spain's side until she regained Gibraltar, the offer was accepted, and late in 1779 relations were severed with England, and Baron Grantham, deceived by Florida Blanca to the last moment, departed in anger for England.

With America, France and Spain united in arms, there was still another blow to fall on the hard-beset British people. It came as a result of the formation of the Armed Neutrality. Acting under the ruling sea-code, the British navy searched neutral ships and seized enemy goods, though freeing the captured ship. Nations with many merchant ships and few war vessels suffered heavily, and began to assert a new doctrine that free ships made free goods, that a neutral ship protected all goods on board. It agreed with the growing humanitarian principle that the interests of peace were first, that the area and influence of war must be limited. The benevolent despots, Frederick and Catherine, took up the idea, but England resisted it as a blow to her sea power. Frederick, eager to avenge what he called England's desertion in 1761, used his influence with Catherine to get her to head a league of armed neutrality which would enforce the new proposed rule of the sea.

Frederick had no desire for war with England, but his wish to injure her led to the curious idea that he had a sentimental friendship for the Americans. An amusing myth grew up that he sent Washington a sword inscribed "From the Oldest General to the Greatest," yet in truth he was a severe critic of Washington's military fitness. Frederick said of the war in America that it was to him amusement like the combats of gladiators of which the Romans sat tranquil spectators. Indeed, he was so busy with Bohemia and Saxony that he "hardly so much as remembered that there were Americans in the world." He refused his ports to German mercenaries on the way to fight America, but that was because he wanted to hire them for his own wars. While England, France and Spain acted on the "bloody stage of Mars" he took pleasure "beholding them tilt and parry with each other." The arms bought in Prussia on his minister's advice proved rotten, and the American protest he treated with ironical amusement. On the whole, his love of America was wholly platonic, but he did make trouble for England, and that was useful.

Beside telling France to go ahead with her revenge upon England, that he would stand aside, Frederick made much trouble through his influence with Panin, the minister of Catherine II. Sir James Harris, with all his diplomatic skill, failed to prevent Catherine's proclamation, the intent of which was to deprive Great Britain of the principal resource that enabled her to stand her ground amid a world of enemies. Harris found in Catherine a masculine force of mind, though her private life, spent with the very dregs of her court, amid a rapid succession of favourites, was utterly relaxed and dissipated. She was an admirer of Charles James Fox, read Beccaria, and knew her Blackstone so well as to have Harris beyond his depth in a discussion of the British Constitution. She admired the Greeks, showed excellent taste in her sumptuous fêtes, so magnificent that Harris speaks of a supper where the jewels adorning the table were valued at £2,000,000. No flattery was too gross to please her. "For God's sake don't be ashamed to flatter her" urged Potemkin. "Her enemies lull her to sleep with praise, she breaks with friends who tell the truth." Allow her in the right though in the wrong, urged Harris' mentor. It was all in vain, however, for though Harris begged daily, from the British Government, money for corruption, and bribed, as every other diplomat did, ladies, secretaries, valets, he found Catherine the "mistress of dissimulation." Just after she had given Harris a golden snuff-box, his wife a diamond necklace, and had even stood godmother to his new-born child, she signed, March 8, 1780, the proclamation utterly against the British interests. Her wish to pose as "the restorer of the freedom of the seas"—the same golden vision that lured President Wilson in our own time— and. what she believed her economic interests, triumphed over her desire for the good of England. Denmark and Sweden, and later other powers, ranged themselves with Russia in what came to be known as the Armed Neutrality. Still, it came near being the "armed nullity," for the chief limitation upon England's power to damage her enemies would come if the leagued neutrals should protect the great carrying trade of the Netherlands. To prevent that, England made the Dutch vulnerable by making them open enemies before they could make up their phlegmatic minds to sign with the armed neutrals.

The Dutch attitude toward the war had naturally been dictated by their interests. The masses were friendly to the colonies from the first, because the struggle seemed analogous to the Dutch struggle with Spain, and they hoped an independent America would open to them new sources of commerce and wealth. The war, indeed, was a gold mine for Dutch trade, which reached heights never gained before. As early as May, 1775, Dutch merchants carrying munitions at their own risks, brought quantities of powder to America. The great base of their operations was the island of St Eustatius in the West Indies until that port was destroyed by Rodney in 1781. But neutrality was most important. "Their High Mightinesses, the Dutch," said Voltaire, "must remain neuter" so they may send "gunpowder and cheese to both states." France, too, turned to them as a chief source of naval stores and provisions. Pressed by Sir Joseph Yorke, the States-General passed a resolution not to let the American vessels have arms, and a little over a year later they issued what amounted to a proclamation of neutrality which was never effective. Since the French encouraged every Dutch act which supplied America's war needs, there grew up bitter French and English factions in the Netherlands. The Prince of Orange, a tool of the English, led one, while Van der Capellan van de Poll led the other, supporting the American cause—"the cause of humankind" as he called it. John Adams, flitting from one Dutch official to another, trying to draw the Dutch into an alliance with America, or to secure recognition, was a sad picture, but we now know that the French preferred the Dutch as neutrals and blocked all American efforts toward an alliance. Adams, therefore, denounced the Dutch as indolent, divided, animated with party spirit, and when seeking a loan compared himself to a man swimming in mid-ocean negotiating for his life with a school of sharks. Yorke, no more successful, called the Dutch "an ungrateful, dirty, senseless people." It was when in this state of mind that the crisis came, the Dutch being on the verge of signing with Catherine the Armed Neutrality agreement. England and the Netherlands had already quarrelled over an old treaty, and Holland had recently offended by sheltering J. Paul Jones after the *Bon Homme Richard* and the *Serapis* affair, when the British captured Henry Laurens carrying a projected Dutch-American treaty signed by the chief magistrate of Amsterdam. The British demanded the punishment of the magistrate, which the States-General had no constitutional power to administer, and upon the failure to comply, war was declared. The Dutch impending accession to the Armed Neutrality was the real reason, but Catherine preferred to believe in the British explanation, and remained neutral. England was then at open war with a jealous world, with her colonies, with France, Spain and Holland, while the armed neutrals menaced her if she used to the full her greatest weapon, sea power.

This was the grand result, not merely of the clash of the diplomatic forces of England and America on the tilting ground of Continental Europe, but of the culmination of policies pursued in some cases through many generations of European peoples. The European war was the resultant of many forces, the ambitions of kings, the pride of nations in their prestige, the economic interests of merchants and traders in many lands, the follies of ministers, the unreasoning hate one people of another, and out of all the welter, the hurly-burly of arms, the intrigues of diplomats came the birth of a new nation, the United States of America. Because France for a brief time could hold command of the sea at the mouth of Chesapeake Bay, the surrender of the British army under Cornwallis was compelled. The blow of that military reverse led to the fall of Lord North's ministry, and the rise to power of Rockingham, Fox and Shelburne, opponents of the war from the first. The policy of these men was best stated by Shelburne when he wrote: "The great object of this country is not merely peace, but reconciliation with America on the noblest terms, and by the noblest means."

INDEX

For EU product safety concerns, contact us at Calle de José Abascal, 56–1°,
28003 Madrid, Spain or eugpsr@cambridge.org.

www.ingramcontent.com/pod-product-compliance
Ingram Content Group UK Ltd.
Pitfield, Milton Keynes, MK11 3LW, UK
UKHW020316140625
459647UK00018B/1905